NOT ANOTHER LECTURE

20 FINBIT$ OF UNSOLICITED Dad Wisdom ABOUT MONEY

JOHNNY BOHAN, CFP®

Not Another Lecture: 20 Finbit$ of Unsolicited Dad Wisdom About Money
Published by Finbits Media LLC.
Littleton, CO

ISBN: 979-8-9869090-0-4
BUSINESS & ECONOMICS / Personal Finance / Money Management

Cover and interior design by Victoria Wolf, wolfdesignandmarketing.com, copyright owned by Johnny Bohan

QUANTITY PURCHASES: Schools, companies, professional groups, clubs, and other organizations may qualify for special terms when ordering quantities of this title. For information, email johnny@johnnypbohan.com.

For Jack, Ellie & Kate ... thank you for enduring my unsolicited Dad wisdom over the years. Hopefully I get to hear you pass that unsolicited wisdom on to my grandkids someday!

CONTENTS

Part IV: Safeguard Yourself and Your Stuff

Part V: Build Your Wealth

FOREWORD
BY JACK

I SUPPOSE I'VE BEEN TASKED with writing this as an endorsement of a personal finance book targeting younger generations. Who is more credible than I, being either one of the youngest Millennials or the oldest of Gen Z, to convince you to read this? And a wise choice by the author to pick his oldest son as a spokesperson. Plenty of personal experience to draw from and unlikely to completely tarnish his reputation.

Don't worry; the whole book may only take you a few hours to read.

I have known my father for twenty-six years. I have been afraid of spending money for at least twenty of them. My other credentials include graduating college in nearly four years, never filing for bankruptcy, and being six foot three with zero athleticism. All of which I can credit to my dad.

I'll be honest: this book is riddled with corny Dad jokes. Like, a lot. You may physically cringe. You may audibly groan. At some points, I wondered if he spent more time researching Millennial stereotypes than financial topics. My advice would be to picture your own dad saying these words out loud to you, and it will start to make a ton of sense. All dads have the same jokes, material from *Caddyshack* and *Christmas Vacation*. Then you'll start to notice that dads only become more like Clark Griswold as they age, and they think the *Vacation* movies are even funnier. Imagining your own dad saying all these jokes may make the words more endearing. Or perhaps you will cringe even harder.

I could tell a hundred stories of my dad's … frugal … habits and covert money-learning opportunities disguised as life lessons. I'll just toss out a few.

Once, he helped me set up a high-yield savings account at my bank. If I locked up my money for a year, it would pay 1.5 percent interest as opposed to the regular 0.003 percent. I probably had $300 and thought it was a great idea. At that rate, I would become a millionaire in 222,222 years.

Back in middle school, we were in the Sonic drive-thru when my dad realized we were fifteen minutes early for the happy hour offering of half-priced slushies. So, he BACKED OUT of the drive-thru line, forcing other cars to do the same. He pulled into a parking spot to wait for the happy hour to start as my sisters and I slunk down in our seats to avoid seeing anybody we knew. All to save maybe four dollars.

On a family vacation to the southern mountains in Colorado, he gave each of us kids $100 to spend throughout the trip. Any extra money we had at the end, we got to keep. How very clever: a lesson in budgeting. We avoided gift shops that weekend.

The stress of it nearly broke my sisters, too worried to spend anything. I also planned on not spending a dime the entire trip, but I was content with my decision. My dad's financial experiment derailed our vacation, but somewhere down deep, it might have taught us to watch what we spend.

My dad has never thrown away a T-shirt. PB&Js are his favorite meal. Adjusting the thermostat for more heat is strictly forbidden. He will drive around town, sometimes for twenty minutes or more, until he finds the cheapest gas station. Any of this starting to sound familiar?

All this to say, my two sisters and I have been the guinea pigs building to the creation of this book. So if you're looking at your life ahead of you and all the boring, practical choices you get to make and all the even more boring ways to financially educate yourself, at least now you have this book as an option. Somehow, my dad packed bits of wisdom on investing, insurance, managing your debt, and more into a rather thin book. If you can look past the goofy façade of the writing, he is still an expert on all of this. And more importantly, he recognizes how horribly dull and intentionally obscure financial topics can be. If anything, this book is a frantic attempt to make all these convoluted topics a little more digestible.

You ever look back at yourself from ten years ago and think about all the stupid decisions you made? Or five years ago? Or last weekend? As my dad or any other adult will tell you, they wish they had started investing and managing their money sooner. I can't guarantee you'll be a personal finance expert after you finish reading, but you will learn a few things and certainly be more aware of your own money habits. And I can promise this will (probably) be the least boring financial book you will read.

INTRO

REMEMBER WHEN YOU BEGGED YOUR DAD to go to
Joey's to play video games for the fifth day in a row? Or you
pleaded with the old man to let you go "hang out" with that "nice"
guy from band practice? Or maybe you just wanted to stay out
past midnight with your harmless, wholesome "church youth
group" friends over at the lake. You were relentless, but he was
not budging. He wasn't buying what you were selling. He shot
down every reason/argument/plea that you threw at him for
hours until he pulled out his final Dad card: "You're not going
BECAUSE I SAID SO!" Game over! He knew he was out of reasons,
and you knew you were S.O.L. (sh.t out of luck).

Let me start by saying I'm probably going to trot out on my
proverbial front lawn and preach a lot in this book. Scratch that. I'm
definitely going to preach a lot. In simple terms, I will explain why
you should do all this financial prep work, and I will give you solid
data to back it up, but in the end, just do it because I said so. You'll
be better off in the long run, and you can thank me in forty years!

Why should you listen to me? I'm a dad of three twenty-somethings, which means I've gone through every scenario in this book either personally or by coaching my young-adult kids. I'm a Certified Financial Planner, which means I have the educational credentials in the personal finance industry and have worked with hundreds of individuals trying to solve these financial puzzles. I'm also a college finance professor, which means I've bored students to tears—I mean, I've taught personal finance to upper-class business students. Did I brag that I have a biweekly true crime podcast that I host called **FINBIT$** with *Johnny B?* Okay, it's not technically a true crime podcast, but I got your attention, and we do tackle these financial issues every week in an entertaining and educational dad kind of way. And finally, I've rotated around on this Earth for over half a century. That last qualification trumps the rest because I've gone through everything I detail in this book.

I initially wrote this book for my three adult-like kids, Jack, Ellie, and Kate. They are starting to experience these financial conundrums, so as I put together the information in this book, I figured *Why not share my unsolicited wisdom with the rest of you!* Yes, you'll have to endure my Dad jokes and sarcasm, but I promise you'll pick up some financial bits of wisdom that will help you throughout your early working years and your growing family years.

Give yourself a participation trophy because you made it. Sixteen years of school, and you're finally a semi-adult. You're now paying your own rent and car insurance. As soon as your dad boots you off his cell phone plan and you have to get your own Netflix login, you know you're a full-blown adult. You can still scroll through your TikTok and Snapchat with your friends at halftime of the football game; however, I'm sorry to say you also have to slog through your benefits paperwork at work and make some selections. Oh, and you have to choose some investment funds for your 401(k), and finally, you have to meal prep on Sunday for the week. Arghhhh, being an adult is hard work! So many decisions and so little interest.

I get it. I have little interest in picking out knick-knacks for our home. I have zero interest in shopping for clothes. I have subzero interest in picking out paint colors for the bathroom. So, I'm going to assume that you have little interest in most things financial. Again, I get it. That is the point of this slim book. The idea is to give you some quick references when you have to make a financial decision because you will, at some point, have to make these decisions.

I'll assume you are finished with your formal schooling. Finito! Did your teachers cram all the stuff in your noggin that you will need to succeed in life? Maybe? Doubtful! I'm fairly confident that you skipped at least one class. It's not English 201 that you'll have a recurring nightmare about when you're forty-two, but the missing class about MONEY. How to get it. How to keep it. How to protect it. How to spend it ... or not spend it, for that matter.

Don't worry; it's not your fault. The Money Class that we all so desperately needed wasn't offered. Sure, you could take a class at Caltech on The Amazing World of Bubbles, but if you wanted to learn about your benefits at work, you were, again, S.O.L. We can look at over 63.5 percent of the class schedules at every major college, and we won't see a class on personal finance—even though it will impact every one of you. Don't worry; your Financial Dad is here to help.

As a dad, I've made some bold statements over the years ...

Are we air-conditioning the whole block?

Don't eat that.

You will finish that!

What the hell were you thinking?

Who are you going out with?

Do you think the trash bag is going to take itself out?

You know it's okay to put gas "in" the car too.

I don't recall saying that.

Go ask your mom!

Obviously, as a dad, I (and every dad I know, for that matter) will give you unlimited and unsolicited opinions on any number of subjects. Yet somehow, we dads have stumbled our way through a boatload of financial decisions. Some of these choices were spot on, and many others were epic failures, but that is the goal of this book. To give you twenty **FINBIT$** of wisdom to help get you started on the right financial trail.

What are **FINBIT$**? They are not devices that track every step you take during the day as you hope to achieve the almighty ten thousand. They are financial bits of information and revelations that I wish someone had pounded into my head in my twenties and thirties. I dare say every adult would tell you that they wish they had started earlier. Saving, eating healthy, budgeting, exercising, investing, and just learning about financial things. Whatever the case may be, most adults wish they had built a basis of knowledge about personal finance and that they had started good habits a lot earlier. Myself included!

Here's what else you need to know about me. I'm your above-average dad. I am six foot four, and most dads are five foot nine. I say that tongue in cheek because all my kids are "above average," which is statistically impossible, but I want to have something to say at the neighborhood barbecue. Against all odds, I convinced my wife to go out with me thirty years ago. We somehow managed to produce and keep alive three young adults who are in college or recent graduates.

I realize that not everyone has had the same experience that I have. I'm lucky, biased, and ignorant of what I have not experienced. Keep all of that in mind while you read this. I'm far from perfect—validated daily, sometimes hourly, by each of my family members—and I've made enough mistakes and bad decisions to fill a book three times this size ("Four," my wife says). But there are some things I can claim as successes. Those kids I mentioned. And a long career in wealth management as a Certified Financial Planner—helping people become and remain financially stable. Get rich slowly!

As a college personal finance professor, I wish I had every student on campus in my class, but for some reason, some students would rather take "Advanced Bowling Strategies" than learn how to manage their money for the rest of their lives. Okay, I admit I took two semesters of bowling in college to round out my electives but only after I completed all my required financial classes, of course!

Trust me, at some point, you will need some or all of these **FINBIT$**, and hopefully this book will trigger a brain synapse for you when you need it. I know you like to argue with Dad, ridicule Dad because of his Costco jeans, and sometimes just flat out ignore Dad. I can take the snarky fashion comments, but when it comes to money, I've got some knowledge that I demand you hear.

At the end of each *finbit*, I'll give you two **GOBIT$**. These aren't complicated financial equations but simple action items to get you going. Commit to one or two, and then start dreaming of traveling to Paris or Thailand or the Ozarks (if that's your sort of thing).

Pause Netflix. Grab your emotional support hydro flask or one of those god-awful cough-medicine-tasting energy bombs and hunker down. Give me a couple of hours to help get you on the right financial path, and then you can impress your friends with your newfound financial fitness.

#financialhumorist
#InDadWeTrust
#finfluencer
#DadisnotasmuchofanidiotasIthoughthewas
#Cheapskatedads
#finbits
#BecauseIsaidso

PART I:
FUNDAMENTALS
Let's Start with the Basics

TEN THOUSAND HOURS. That's what they say. No, it's not to get through TSA at the airport but to master the guitar. Or to perfect your tennis swing. Or to learn how to mine bitcoin. Okay, I made that last one up, but I'm sure mining crypto will take a while. Ten thousand hours of grinding out the fundamentals to master a particular skill. Four hundred seventeen days of consistent practice to master a skill like tennis, dance, or quantum theory. Did I scare you off yet?

Don't worry; I'm not asking you to dedicate ten thousand hours to learning about personal finance, but I am asking—no, scratch that—I'm begging you to learn the fundamentals. Learn the basics, and I promise you, they will guide you for the rest of your financial life.

When I was in fifth grade, I had to make a life-changing decision. Back home in Prairie Village, Kansas, our football team was unstoppable. We crushed every other Catholic school in town, and I loved it. I loved practice. I loved game day. The only thing is that the coaches didn't love me. At age twelve, I was a backup offensive lineman. For some reason, at five foot ten and 100 lb. soaking wet, I didn't get a lot of playing time. You see, linemen tend to be a little thicker, and I was so skinny I'd blow over in the wind. What I lacked in speed and strength, I countered with a lack of raw talent. Damn I loved football, but the game just didn't love me back. I picked up a tennis racket at the same time and decided it was time to take my talents to the hard courts. Little did I know the dedication the tennis court would demand from me.

YouTube didn't exist back in the eighties, so I learned the game by pounding the ball against a backboard at the public courts. I hit against that freakin' wall for hours and then eventually played against some freckled kid who was smacking the wall one court over. I went on to play junior tournaments and had modest success in high school. Unfortunately, this doesn't end with me beating Rafa Nadal at the French Open, but I think I crushed Billy Criqui at the Twelve and Under PV Invitational. "What's the point?" you wonder as you roll your eyes at my extended tennis saga. Back when I was twelve, I drilled the fundamentals and put in the thousands of hours that allowed me to play today. Forty years later, I'm still swinging a racket with my buddies. A little slower, but my forehand is almost identical to what it was back in the day. Erratic but awesome every tenth time it lands inside the lines!

I don't have to think about how to crush a forehand. It is automatic muscle memory, and that is what I want your thoughts about money to become. Learn the **FUNdamentals** over the next four chapters, and they will shape your bank account for decades. Form the right habits for handling your money, and it will help reduce the stress of daily financial decisions. Why? Because I said so!

I'm awesome with directions. Watch this: "Hey Google, find the nearest Chipotle." Bam! Done—0.75 miles away. My phone says I can walk there in twelve minutes. I guess I could order online and go pick it up? Or ... Order online and have it delivered? Absolutely. But when my dad reminds me to go find a place to change the oil thingy on my car, I get sleepy. For some reason, my dad always interrogates me about my car and my money. How's your bank balance? Did you change the wipers? Where are you at with your budget? How do the tires look? I'm an independent woman, and I know what I'm doing with my money and my car, I think. Do you think he's planning a hostile takeover of my finances?

Signed, "I am Olivia. Hear me roar!"

Dear "I am Olivia!"

Whoa! Good for you for kinda sorta knowing where you are going. Don't worry; it's your dad's job to worry about windshield wipers, money in the bank, and if your car tires are properly inflated. Even though you're out on your own, it never hurts to have the old man look over your shoulder. With your busy life, Pops wants to check in on your finances and your car because he's terrified to ask about your girlfriend drama and your sometimes live-in boyfriend. Let him stick to checking in on things he understands, like all-season tires versus asking if your boyfriend has a toothbrush at your apartment. Having your Pops check in with you about your career, your financial picture, and the tread life on your car tires once in a while will make him happy that he's contributing to your adulthood!

Chapter 1

DROP A PIN!
Where Are You Right Now?

"I'm stuck between 'I need to
save money' and 'YOLO.'"

— Everyone

GOOGLE IT! DROP A PIN! OPEN A MAP?! Just kidding, nobody's opened a map since Dad asked Mom to find Winfield, Kansas, when he was driving the whole crew in the family truckster to Disneyland way back in the eighties.

Where are you today? Back when I was your age (this is the first of seventy-three times I will use this phrase), we didn't have smartphones, Google, Siri, or bottled water, for that matter. We had to physically open a map, find our destination, and drink tap water. And then (this will sound crazy), we had to plot our

path to get there. However, to know where to go, you had to first find yourself on the map. Kind of like when you're lost in Ikea, and you look for the "You Are Here" icon on the store map. (If you can even find a store map at Ikea. I think they intentionally hope you get lost, and then you'll be forced to buy an unassembled cabinet to escape the furniture maze, but you'll eventually have to return the cabinet because the directions are written in Swedish, and your brain hurts too much to figure it out. Okay I'm done with that rant, although I do love their meatballs!) I think you see where I'm going with this. Mapping out your personal finances is not terribly difficult, but much like planning a hike in the mountains, staying on the right path and adjusting for adverse conditions are musts.

HEY JOHNNY B, WHY SHOULD I CARE?

Valid question. You will notice that I have a lot of conversations with myself in the book, but really, I'm channeling questions that I have received from my kids or other young adults, and I assume you may have the same questions. As you repeatedly heard in high school biology, there are no dumb questions. Maybe there are dumb questions in high school, but when it comes to your money and what to do with it, there are definitely no dumb questions. This is why you should care!

Let's pause a moment and pat yourself on the back for starting to think a smidgen about your personal financial picture by reading this book. Maybe Santa stuffed it in your stocking at Christmas, or Aunt Theresa dropped it on your gift table at your wedding, or Mom slipped this little book of financial wisdom into your travel luggage. Since you've opened it, you're ahead of 90 percent of your peers in taking ownership of your finances. Ninety is a percentage that seems about right from my informal polling of ten Millennials.

The fact is most young adults, or any adults, for that matter, aren't too thrilled about exploring their personal finances. Texting back and forth with your girlfriends about why Hudson got booted off *The Bachelorette* is infinitely more interesting than researching your work benefits. I kind of get it. However, making conscious decisions about your personal finances can impact your well-being more than whether you should start Mahomes or Allen on your fantasy football team. Chances are, you've got some goals and dreams that depend on you being financially sound. At the very least, on you being financially aware of what's happening around you. What I'm saying is if you have a good handle on your finances, you can do the stuff you want to do!

According to a recent study from Fidelity entitled the Millennial Money Study ... wow, they really got creative with that title ... here are Millennials' top financial concerns:

- 52 percent want to accumulate more savings for retirement
- 41 percent want to pay off credit card debt
- 28 percent want to pay off student loans[1]

And 17 percent are nervous about what they posted on social media last night.

Even though that last stat is somewhat embellished, I'm confident that 17 percent is probably low! Do you fall into one of these categories? Do you fall into all these categories? Or is your primary concern to save enough to quietly quit your current job and backpack the Appalachian Trail for six months?

Money is just a utility so you can buy stuff, go places, repay loans, and live as you want. Your feelings about money will certainly evolve at various times in your life, but ultimately, you have control of your behavior toward financial issues. Dare I repeat myself: *You* have total control over how you react to financial issues.

On a random side note, two-thirds of Millennials think it is more acceptable now for children to move back to their parents' homes after college. A separate unofficial poll of fellow parents I know suggests 100 percent of us love our kids but don't want them moving back into the basement. Hence why we, as parents of Millennials, should vacate the home for a camper van and make it difficult to find us. My wife is not on board with this idea—yet!

Most people let money decisions overwhelm them, and then they bury their heads in the sand, hoping the bad decisions auto-correct. You've seen how your phone auto-corrects your texts and how that can go horribly wrong. What if you forget to pay your monthly credit card bill? The bank hits you with 25 percent interest charges and late fees. What if you don't save money for emergencies? Suddenly, the transmission goes out on your old SUV, or a separated shoulder from a mountain bike endo (tumbling over the handlebars and crashing) sends you to the ER. These expenses add up. If you don't have an emergency fund, then you'll have to borrow from your credit card, and that could lead to high interest charges. And finally, what if you don't save consistently at an early age for retirement? Instead of taking exotic European river cruises in retirement, you may be living in a van down by the river.

If you can anticipate your needs and income, then you are better equipped to make decisions. So, saddle up, and let's get started.

KEEP IT SIMPLE

Financial planning ... kinda makes you vurp a little in your mouth when you say it out loud. Very few individuals want to do financial planning, and if they do, it's hard to convince your significant other to complete the perceived torture with you. Think of it as if you were planning a hike. I'm not talking about an expedition up Mount Everest or even tackling a fourteener in Colorado, like Pikes Peak. Let's call it a reasonable five-miler with streams, some wildlife, and a cliff or two. Where do you want to go? Where is the trailhead? How long will it take? How could the weather impact your hike? Same goes for your personal finances. Where are you today? Where do you want to go? What could derail your plans?

If this were my college personal finance class, the students and I would be diving into balance sheets, income statements, time value of money, debt ratios, and macroeconomic theory. **Please NOT another lecture, Dad!** Fine, just give me a few moments. Whether you are running a business or running your life, you must first figure out what money is coming in and what is going out. How much do you have today? How much do you owe today? How much do you make each month? How much do you spend each month?

There are many useful tools to figure this out, and I've included an example of a balance sheet and an income statement, but you can certainly start with a Big Chief tablet (my personal favorite from my kindergarten years), iPad notes, spiral notebook, your bank's app, or the back of your latest return shipping label.

STEP 1: Organize your stuff on a Balance Sheet

List what you have and what you owe, a.k.a. stuff you own that someone else might think is worth something, and loans that you have to pay back or the lender will hunt you down to the ends of the earth. If you're old-school and writing this down, just draw a line across the top and then a line down the middle of a blank paper. Write "Assets" on the left side of the ledger and "Liabilities" on the right. Write down the name of the asset; for example, your slick 2000 Gold Honda Accord, and your long-term liabilities; for example, a student loan from your pursuit of a degree in Advanced Sociology of the Mountain Lion from Colorado State U. List everything you think is relevant and attach an estimated dollar amount. If you know the amount of your liability payments, when they are due, and when the loans will be paid off, that will be helpful, too.

Personal Balance Sheet

Your Stuff	$$	Your Debt	$$
Cash	$2,500	Loan – Grandma Gretchen	$1,500
Stand-Up Paddleboard	$1,200	Student Loans	$22,000
SUV	$22,000	Car Loan	$12,000
Townhouse	$350,000	Mortgage	$275,000
Vintage Ukulele	$500	Credit Card Balance	$1,200
Xbox	$23	Venmo Requests	$65

STEP 2: Build your Income Statement

Next up is assembling your income statement. Don't get dizzy. I'm not asking for complicated financial ratios but simply what money comes into your bank account each month and what goes out. At this early stage in your life, the money coming in is probably simple and is your income from your job. Don't count your Dunkin' Rewards or Lululemon gift cards as income (though they are nice to have). If you have a side gig as a nanny, Uber Eats driver, or website developer, then add that to your income column. Your expenses should be the monthly items that you have to pay, or the companies you owe will call you relentlessly to demand payment.

Monthly Personal Income Statement

Incoming	$$	Outgoing	$$
Salary – Monthly	$6,000	Rent	$1,500
Bonus – monthly	$500	Credit Card	$1,000
Side Hustle	$500	Utilities	$200
Dividends & Interest	$100	Car Payment	$500
		Emergency Fund	$100
		Taxes, Insurance	$1,000

Okay, I threw a lot at you in Chapter 1. The idea is to get a handle on where you are financially. If you start to track your income and expenses, then you are way ahead of your fantasy football league opponents. Find a system that works for you and develop a "base case" of where you are today. Don't jump into investing, loan research, or car buying until you can pinpoint your current financial situation. All right, that's enough dad preaching for one chapter.

As I mentioned in the intro, at the end of each **FINBIT**, I'll give you two action items. I've called them **GO-BIT$** because you just need to go do them. These aren't suggestions to consider or ideas for you to give a half-ass attempt. Do them! Much like your dad when you were little, I'm going to try to explain why you should do all this stuff, but in the end, just do them ...

... because I said so.

≡GOBIT$

GO-BIT #1: Go old-school and sketch out a budget sheet or download a budget spreadsheet from Google Docs or Excel, similar to what I've included in the Appendices. Keep it simple. Or you can find a budget app at your financial institution or at mint.com. The key is to find something that works for you, get going, and stick to it.

GO-BIT #2: Track your income and expenses. In other words, fill in the numbers. By downloading a spreadsheet or financial app, you have completed Step 1. Start with your income minus taxes. What is your take-home pay every week or every two weeks? Track your expenses for one week. Then track for one month. And then track for three months. It can be challenging the first few months, but it gets easier. Turn it into a habit. If you don't know the exact expense total for a category, give it your best estimate and aim high. Don't sandbag your expenses, which means don't underestimate what you really spend. After three months of tracking expenses, you'll have a pretty good idea of what you regularly spend. If you put most of your purchases on a card, then go to your bank website, and it will organize them in categories for you.

I love Brad. I admit it. We are very close, and I don't know where I'd be without Brad, my phone. Yes, I named him Brad! Sometimes, my buddy Brad hides from me in my couch cushions or under the driver's seat, but he always shows up. I can't say the same about my soon-to-be-ex boyfriend. He's about as reliable as dial-up internet. Brad has been a super helpful buddy to help keep me on track with my workouts, sleep time, and music choices. Do you think Brad can help me manage my money better?

Signed,

Brad's #1 Fan

Dear FOB (friend of Brad),

You may need to spend a little alone time away from Brad. It's a piece of plastic, not a human, but you're not alone in your mild obsession. If you really need help managing your finances, technology can help get you organized, but you might consider finding a true buddy who has similar interests as you. Having someone to share your money victories and failures with is a great way to learn new ideas. Go crazy and find another human who may have similar financial issues, and you may start to loosen the connection with Brad.

Chapter 2

FIND YOUR MONEYBUDDY

"Hey buddy, I know your girlfriend is
ghosting you, but do you want to hang out
and talk about your money situation?"

— Said nobody ever ... but they should

"GOOOOOOOOAAAAALLLLLLLLLLLLLLLLLL!!!"

Can you hear the call echoing between your ears? It's that
Telemundo soccer announcer who yells for some ungodly
amount of time. If you haven't seen or, more likely, heard it,
then YouTube it. World Cup Soccer Announcer Andrés Cantor
has made a name for himself over the last thirty years by turning
a normal game call into the most exciting moment in sports.
Soccer, a.k.a. fútbol, is a worldwide obsession, and the outcome
hinges on a goal here or there during the match. Famed foot-
baller Lionel Messi showed this obsession to the world in the
2022 World Cup by striking the go-ahead goal for Argentina

and leading his home country to their first World Cup in three decades.

How does that translate into your financial life? Well, it may not be as dramatic as a World Cup goal, but you should have a GOAL! Or several goals and a buddy to help you check them off. I'm not saying you'll scream "GOOOAAALLL!" every time you and your MoneyBuddy accomplish goals, but maybe a random cartwheel isn't out of the question when you check one off your list.

SET IT BUT DON'T FORGET IT

Setting goals is easy. Taking those first steps toward your goals is scary. Not like "I failed to turn in my history paper senior year in college because we decided to play Ultimate frisbee all weekend and I have an hour to write it" scary, but still. Nobody wants to set a goal and then fail miserably.

Ninety-two percent of people who set New Year's goals never achieve them, according to a study by University of Scranton.[2] Of those 92 percent, only half, 46 percent, still pursued those goals six months later. So, the odds are stacked against us. But with a buddy, you increase your chances of success. Last year, two of my adult-ish kids, Jack and Ellie, had a goal to run the half marathon in Chicago in October. For non-runners like me, that sounds awful, but for them, it puts a target on the calendar. To be ready, they started training in January. Even though they were a thousand miles apart, they became workout buddies. Ellie downloaded a running workout schedule that would help them build up to the race. Jack bought some new socks. They didn't need a spreadsheet or scheduled video chats. A simple threatening text each week was sufficient to coerce each other to lace up and hit the pavement.

"Hey Jack, I'm running 5 mi Wed, 7 mi Sat, and then 3 mi on Monday!"

"Hey Ellie, I don't care. Oh, and I ran 6 mi yesterday."

"Yah well, I ran 42 miles in January."

"I ran 15 mi. Skied 6 days and 'toured' 7 breweries."

"You're an idiot. And good job big bro!"

"You smell funny. Keep it up lil sis!"

Sibling banter can be so charming and much more vulgar, but I'm trying to keep this at least PG-13. A workout buddy will increase your success by 67.3 percent, according to some health magazine that I can't seem to locate. Same goes for a MoneyBuddy. Having an accountability partner will help keep you both on track. The term "accountability partner" seems too formal, like you're an intern at a CPA firm, so I went with MoneyBuddy.

STEP #1: CHOOSE SOMEONE YOU ACTUALLY WANT TO TALK TO

"Great!" you mumble to yourself. "Now I have to find a buddy! It feels like we are pairing up for the lab experiment in high school and my options are down to Helen or Ricky Bobby."

Find a buddy who will actually check in with you and that you want to talk to. I can't stress this enough. College buddy. Work buddy. Family member. Someone in a similar financial situation would be ideal.

Sounds simple, but maybe your mom isn't the ideal buddy because she'll listen but also let you skate by if you don't try very hard. "Good try, sweetie! I'm sure you'll do better next month." Your ex-military neighbor could be ideal for holding you accountable, but then Sergeant Hulka might bang on your door every morning at 5:00 a.m., which may be a little much. "Up and at 'em, maggot! Where's this week's budget you promised me?!" Find a reasonable friend who wants to play along, and plan to visit about financial things once a month. It could be your skiing buddy Annie, or it could be your fishing pal Delaney. Try it out for three months and make a change if needed. If Delaney is annoying and just brags about how her fish catches are all way bigger than yours but doesn't ask about your money achievements, then cast her aside and find another MoneyBuddy.

STEP #2: MAKE IT A DATE

You now have a MoneyBuddy. What's next? Create an accountability calendar for when you will meet, text, video, tandem bike, sleigh ride, yoga, or chat on the ski lift. Whatever your plan of interaction, make it consistent and have fun.

"Hey Ella, can you quiz me about my financial goals each Saturday since we are stuck in traffic driving home from another bluebird day on the slopes?"

"Sure, Maeve, and I'm super stoked to tell you about my budgeting process and how I'm socking so much away in my Roth IRA!"

Okay, maybe the conversation isn't quite that dorky and energetic, but you know what I mean. Don't make it complicated but do make it consistent. Plan on once a month, same day, same time for six months. The first meeting may include a few glasses of wine or a hamburger and fries, but going forward it may just be a text, Snapchat, FaceTime, smoke signal, or whatever social platform has taken over the world when you read this.

SO, ABOUT THOSE GOALS ...

How do you set goals that won't embarrass you, are within the realm of possibility, and will result in your financial improvement? Don't freak out. Start simple. A Lamborghini and château in Aspen are goals but may not be realistic if your current transportation is a hand-me-down scooter and you live on your bro's couch. It's good to dream and dream big, but let's start with some short- and mid-term goals that will help you get going. Remember, in Chapter 1, we tried to figure out where you are today. The next step is goal-setting. Here are potential goals to consider:

GOOOOOAAAAALLLLLSSSSS

1. Find a MoneyBuddy.

2. Eliminate credit card debt.

3. Find a higher-paying remote job that I can do in my jammies.

4. Take an annual lake trip with high school buds.

5. Save money for a down payment on a home purchase.

6. Max out retirement savings each year.

7. Get insured.

8. Jumpstart an emergency fund.

Whatever your goals might be, write them down. Show them to your MoneyBuddy, rank them, and pin them to your shirt like your "homework" when you came home from kindergarten. I suppose you could tape them to your bathroom mirror, set alerts on your phone, or superglue a Post-it to your favorite water bottle. Do whatever keeps them top of mind for you. Finally, create a list of steps for each goal. If you know that an annual excursion will cost you $2,400, then you need to save $200 per month. Or about $50 per week. Divert that money from your paycheck into a savings account and go on to the next goal. You'll never miss that money, and you'll be building up your "Sh.t Happens!" fund that we'll discuss in Chapter 7. Once you write down the goal, share it with your MoneyBuddy, review it monthly, and course-correct if needed. Again, I could throw in statistics on goal-setting and using a system like the 4 P's or S.M.A.R.T., but you already know what to do.

STEP #3: GET 'ER DUN!

Just do it! Act now. Take the bull by the horns. Put one foot in front of the other. No sooner said than done. And my personal favorite, "A stitch in time saves nine." No clue what that means, but since Grandma Gretchen throws it out every so often, it must mean just get started, now! Whatever gets you out of your bean bag chair and motivates you to start on your goals. Share a reward each month with your MoneyBuddy, like a nice meal that doesn't include a drive-thru. Or maybe a new pair of shoes that will also offset your carbon footprint. Or buy your dad a new golf club with your extra savings because of his endless, unsolicited, and spot-on financial advice. Actually, don't buy Dad any clubs because he has too many already. Get something for Mom because we all know she deserves it more. Just tell your dad you are setting financial goals, and you may see tears of joy stream down his face like when his team won the national championship and, of course, when you were born.

STEP #4: STRETCHHHHHHH ....

Stretch goal-setting. You've mastered the weekly "save money" trick and the "spend less" gimmick, and now it's time to invest for the long haul. Beware of the headlines! *Five stocks you shouldn't hold in the next recession. Five reasons to comb your hair to the left. Three reasons crypto is king. How to beat the market 87 percent of the time!* All but one of these headlines were flooding the internet this past week. The headlines you did not see were: *Build a plan. Stay the course. Stretch for your goals.* Do you want a home in the Bahamas? Do you want to make enough money to quit your day job and volunteer 24/7 on projects to save the Earth's water supply? Do you want to own four rental properties by the time you're thirty-five? Do you want to retire at forty, ride your bike across the country, travel the world, and save the planet, all at once? Let's figure out how to push your goals over the finish line!

In the coming chapters, we'll dig in the weeds a little more to help you build and protect your impending wealth.

GOBIT$

GOBIT #3: Find a MoneyBuddy you like. Don't overthink it. It's not that type of commitment. Who cares if your MoneyBuddy is a classic rock fan or chews their nails? Try it out for three months, and if they are not the right person, move on. Plan a time and place to meet. Start today!

GOBIT #4: Define your goals, both immediate goals and stretch goals. For example: Reduce debt. Start a budget. Find a new job. Save 10 percent per paycheck. Plan for a vacation. Save for retirement. Read something financial each week. Brainstorm all the goals you can think of and then pair them down with your MoneyBuddy. Don't freak out. Start with three goals, and then check in with your MoneyBuddy each month to see how both of you are doing. Make it a game, and the one doing better each week gets a complimentary glass of wine, foot rub, or KitKat bar or gets to witness the runner-up attempting fifteen pushups. I'll leave the wager up to you.

I'm a little bigger than some of the other dudes I know. Some would say I'm larger than life. Some would just say I'm just large. Okay I'm fat. Should I go on one of those cleanses and start on one of those fancy diets? Also, I spend a lot of money on food and stupid stuff. Maybe I should go on a spending cleanse too. Whatcha think?

Signed,

Big Boned

Dear Big Boned,

I'm sure you're not fat but maybe a little soft around the edges. I'm not a dietitian or personal trainer, but cutting out the Baconator for breakfast is a start. As far as a financial cleanse, it is a good idea for all of us to hit the reset button every three months. I won't preach about a budget to you, but becoming financially aware of every dollar you spend will open your eyes and maybe influence your food plans.

Chapter 3

BE A CHEAPSKATE

"To retire like a king, live like a college student."

— Johnny B

OKAY, NOW WE KNOW WHERE you are financially. Great start. Here's a blue ribbon. Pet rock. Burrito gift card. Whatever you need to acknowledge your first achievement. If you haven't gathered already, I'm a bit of a smartass, so go ahead and roll your eyes like my kiddos and let me know when you're back on board. Go tell your friends you're getting all adulty and you are working on your personal financial plan. Watch them scatter. Now it's time to proudly become a cheapskate!

Proclaim it loudly from the mountaintop, or at least text somebody in ALL CAPS. Why? Well ... because you can. If you really want to jumpstart your path toward more wealth, the one thing you can most definitely control is your spending. Start now. Seriously, like the next time you are ready to hit the red PURCHASE button on your phone, ask yourself, "Am I really getting a great deal?" How else can I say it? Channel your inner dad!

Remember back in college when you were about to drink that trash can punch at the random house party, and you thought, "Would Mom want me to drink this?" And most (but not all) of the time, you listened to that inner Mom voice. "Don't drink it, honey, you don't know what's in there, and you have a paper to write tomorrow!" Good thing you didn't listen to your inner dad voice. "Free booze! Cool!" Well, now it's time to listen to your inner dad voice. Can I find this cheaper? Do I really need the brand name? I think gas was two cents cheaper around the corner. Can a little bit more web surfing find me a better deal? You bet it can, and again, you'll make Papa proud when you share a story with him about your newfound cheapness.

Whatever you want to call us—frugal, tightwad, Grandpa Denny, bargain hunter, Uncle Dan, penny pincher, miser, thrifty, or just cheapskate, it's one of the most heartwarming phrases you can say to your old man. Of course, right behind "Dad, I got a job," "Dad, I found my own apartment," "Dad, I'm not pregnant," and "Dad, why are you so freakin' cheap?" You may think you are insulting us, but we wear it as a badge of honor. Sure, it's gratifying to make money and watch it grow with smart investments, but if I can sweet talk a server into a plate of wings at half-off happy hour prices when happy hour ended twenty minutes ago, I'm a winner! Sure, my family is cringing in the restaurant booth, but secretly they love my negotiating tactics as they devour the discounted wings.

Obvious Ways to Be Cheap (in no particular order)

- Order water as an appetizer.

- Drive an extra three blocks to save three cents on gas.

- Roll down the windows instead of using AC.

- Cram all your luggage into a carry-on.

- Cut the cord from cable.

- Research the best cell phone deal.

- Air dry your clothes instead of using the dryer.

- Water down your box wine.

CHEAPSKATE-ISM IS A WAY OF LIFE

Being cheap isn't a one-time event. It's a way of life. It's a game. Deep down, dads are competitive animals. I want to win at anything and everything, including cornhole, Candyland, and thumb wrestling, but most of my victories are ancient history. If I can get free delivery on a washer/dryer, or free car mats with my truck purchase, or a $1 discount on my $10 haircut with an expired coupon, I'm ecstatic. Winner, winner, chicken dinner! I will high-five every grandma and toddler to share in my cheapness victory. The other day on my weekly trek to Costco to look for jeans, I discovered they now have free air for your car tires. Can you believe it? Not only is it the cheapest gas in town, but now I can fill up my tires for free and avoid that annoying $2 for air at the gas station. It's the little victories. It's a game. And it's not that hard to win. You just have to play. Unfortunately, moms don't always share the same enthusiasm for undying cheapism. They don't necessarily appreciate cramming their entire wardrobe into a carry-on to avoid baggage charges or waiting in the snow for the Lyft surge prices to calm down to get a better rate. It's a Dad Thing.

Being a cheapskate means that sometimes you must walk away from a deal. It's just not good enough. I'm a little demented because I am one of the few people who enjoys the car-buying process with a car dealer. Later in the book, we'll go deeper into buying a car, but let me tease you a little about the process. I recently wanted to buy a pickup that I had found on the car dealer lot, and it was time to battle with the salesperson and his "hidden" sales manager until I got the price I wanted. The salesperson tried the ole "We have a one-low-price, no-haggle buying process." Maybe that's the process for your standard urban latte-drinking, kale-smoothie metrosexual, but it's not for this Cheap Dad. After several weeks and countless stubborn walkouts of the dealership, the sales manager called me and gave me his "final final-final price." That's all I wanted. He proceeded to tell me to come in and buy the truck the next day or never come within a hundred miles of his dealership again. Victory! I'm not trying to make friends with the sales rep; I just want the absolute best price. And, of course, I want free car mats, but not that undercoating spray sham thingy they try to sell you. We'll talk more about car-buying strategies in Chapter 11.

ALWAYS GET THE BEST DEAL

Today, the frugal factor is less confrontational, which suits most people, but as a Cheapskate Dad, it's pretty lame, if you ask me. The in-person price battle is disappearing, and for most, it's easier because you can use your phone. Since you're on your phone texting, watching puppy videos, and trolling celebrities anyway, you might as well use that little gadget to be a cheapster. You can dump your boyfriend and haggle for a discount all on your phone. Never miss an opportunity to save a few bucks and rid yourself of some dead weight along the way.

I'd like to say there is a process for being cheap, but really, it has to take over your everyday buying emotion. For dads, it's easy. We hate spending money on anything and everything! Gas, eggs, socks, carry-on luggage, appliance delivery, streaming services that don't include sports, and of course, parking. For you, it will take some effort to question everything—nearly everything. No need to question your dad's cargo shorts, black socks, and cross-trainers. He knows his fashion choices are sketchy, but he doesn't care. Question every purchase, and if you decide to pull the trigger, question the price. Ask yourself, "Should I be paying less for this?"

As you can see, no elaborate planning is involved, nor much thought at all to being cheap, which is why dads are so good at it. It's a way of life, and eventually, it will be habit-forming. Somewhere down the road, your own kids will cringe at your outward display of cheapness, and you will smile and think of Pop.

The ultimate victory for a father is when you witness a beautiful display of cheapness from your offspring. My college daughter, Ellie, refuses to pay the $2.75 for each load in the dryer. "Dad, that's like nine bucks to dry my clothes. That's a sub sandwich, chips, and a cookie!" She chooses to spread her wet clothes around her apartment until they dry. Not to be outdone, my daughter Kate recently showed me her new leggings that she bought at T.J. Maxx on sale *with* a coupon. And last but not least, my son, Jack, is twenty-five and drives a twenty-year-old gold Honda, a.k.a. "Goldie," that he inherited from his Grandma Gretchen. He's a productive member of society, lives outside the family compound, and is close to leaving my health plan. His buddies have swanky new SUVs, but he doesn't see the point. "Why do I want to worry about scratches, or spilling my Mickey D's, or it getting stolen? If it's not there in the morning, I'll hop the light rail." Excuse me for a moment. I get emotional when my kids exhibit profound cheapness. I'm so proud.

Early in your career, you may not have much control over your salary or how much you can save, but you can always control your cheapness. It's not hard, but it does take discipline. It's a mindset. It's a way of life.

=GOBIT$

GOBIT #5: Find a cheapskate to emulate, a true hall-of-fame cheapass. You know you have one in your life. Your dad. Your grandpa. Your uncle. I know your mom or grandma may be frugal, which is cute. But I'm talking about a truly demented cheap S.O.B. Take them out for breakfast and ask for their best stories about finding that perfect deal. Plant yourself for a few hours because there will be a lot of them. Don't go to Starbucks, or you'll ruin your credibility. Go to McDonald's and get the senior discount. They'll be thrilled. And, of course, you'll have to buy the meal because they're cheap.

GOBIT #6: Start today! Keep track of your savings. What bargain can you unearth today and for the week? Don't worry about an exotic plan. Just be cheap. Analyze every purchase you make. Should I get the large, or will a medium do? Can I use this BOGO coupon for a free burrito even though it expired last month? Should I drive that extra block or two to save three cents on a gallon of gas? Tally your savings at the end of the month and play against your friends, or really challenge yourself and compete with your Cheap Dad.

Pay yourself first. Pay yourself first. My Grandma Rosie won't stop yapping about it to me. So, I did. I Venmo-d myself $500, and I went out and bought a new smartphone. Will Grandma Rosie be proud of me and open the cookie jar as my reward?!

Signed,

Luv Them Cookies

Dear Luv Them Cookies,

Doubtful; she may hide the cookie jar from you. And you certainly don't want to mess with Grandma's cookie allotment. Mmmm, monster cookies, gingerbread cookies, and chocolate chip cookies right out of the oven with a cold glass of milk. Yumm ... Sorry, I got distracted. Paying yourself first doesn't mean go buy yourself something; it means saving first. When you first get out of school, I'm guessing you are making dramatically more than you did at Domino's in high school. Your expenses went up, too, but you should have some funds left over from each paycheck. First, pay yourself. Which means setting up an automatic deposit from your paycheck to a savings account. It can be $10, $100, or $1,000 per paycheck. Build up that side account and become a Supersaver. Do as Grandma says, and cookies you shall receive!

Chapter 4
ROBO YOUR SAVINGS

"Do not save what is left after spending
but spend what is left after saving."

— Warren Buffett (billionaire rich guy,
legendary investor, cheapskate)

YOU WAKE UP. Fumble around for your phone. Check your
Instagram, TikTok, and other socials. You try not to watch sibling
prank videos, but you do. And finally, you scroll through your
missed texts and chats. After you have sufficiently made an effort
to reconnect with the world, you stumble to the coffeemaker
and start your day. You don't think about it; you just do it, like
brushing your teeth and slipping on your Skechers. Okay, I know,
if you're under fifty, you don't wear Skechers, but if you want true
comfort, you'd nab a pair and not tell your friends.

You do some things in life on autopilot. When you get in your
car, you pull on your seat belt, get directions on your maps, and
queue up the **FINBIT$** *with Johnny B* podcast. Okay, that's wish-
ful thinking and a shameless plug, so realistically, it's a murder/

mystery podcast or one continuous EDM song, but you see where I'm going. That seems to be the order we are used to, and you don't think about it; you just do it. What if you could set up your savings account in the same way? What if you could make saving money a habit like meal prepping on Sunday night? You can and you should. That's right—because I said so! Now you're catching on.

AUTOPILOT YOUR SAVINGS

Remember a few chapters back when we started by getting financially organized, defining financial goals, and exhibiting profound cheapness? With your newfound organization, hopefully you're starting to think that maybe you could find a little bit of extra cash to stash away.

I know you have a lot of needs and wants competing for a share of your wallet (a.k.a. money clip, purse, or debit card). Student loans, rent, shoes, 401(k), and an occasional meal at a place that doesn't have a drive-thru. In Chapters 1 and 2, we covered how to gauge where you are today and set goals. Chapter 3 was about how to embrace cheapness, and now I would add that you can save a little money for the future. Maybe you're in your first real job and you're newly married with that first rescue mutt named Duke and you have baby #1 on the way, and you feel there is no possible way you can find any money to save. YOU CAN! And you must! Because I SAID SO! I feel like lightning should strike from the sky to snap you to attention, or I should crack a ruler to the back of your noggin to get you started (sorry, I was reminiscing about my brutal grade school teacher Sister Kilmarten). Let's carve out $10, $100, or $1,000 per month from your paycheck and watch it grow.

PAYCHECK
- Savings
- Food
- Rent
- FUN

"When I was your age" should be the start of everything a dad says. Most of the time, we have no valid reasoning or understanding about why words are coming out of our mouths, but that doesn't stop us from giving our opinions. What does this have to do with automating your savings practices, or what I call "robo-ing"? It's the revelation I had once I was out from under my dad's roof that maybe he wasn't such an idiot all the time. I realized that despite my father's exaggerated high school athletic accomplishments, he was right. Most of the time. Sure, he was way off on fashion, girls, politics, and macroeconomic drivers, but he nailed it about saving early and often.

The average American started saving for retirement at age "Way TOO LATE." I could find a stat that says the average age is twenty-seven-ish, but trust me, the age is much higher.

As a seasoned, twenty-three-year-old potential TikTok phenom, you might look at that stat above and think, Twenty-seven sounds early to me! I've got years to blow through my cash *like a first-round draft pick!* Number one, TikTok isn't going to make you rich. My unsubstantiated estimate while perusing unlikely dance trios is that .00125 percent of TikTok influencers make a living off their posts. Yes, you're more likely to win the lottery, unwrap a golden ticket from Willy Wonka, or find your soulmate on Love Island. Meanwhile, most non-delusional people can set themselves up for life by starting to save as early as possible.

Aim for twenty-one, the age you might be if you successfully complete college in four-ish years. Twenty-two or -three for those who might take a gap year or are trying their best to get the full college experience in, say, six years. If you're approaching your advancing years like your thirties, then hop aboard the saving-for-retirement train now! Once you're out in the world, here are a few ways to save automatically with little to no effort.

SAVE WITHOUT BREAKING A SWEAT

1. Pay yourself first, then pay your bills

Write a check to yourself like it was your cable bill and deposit it in a savings account. *Hey JB, this isn't the 1980s! Bon Jovi is like sixty years old now; I don't have checks, and I cut the cable cord in college.* I tricked you; I was just trying to get your attention. I guess you could Venmo yourself, but I'm not sure that would really be saving! Plan to save money first before you pay your first bill. Proceed to Step #2!

2. Set up a payroll deduction

You can have your employer deduct money from your paycheck directly into your savings account. No checks. No stamps. No pain because you never see the money. No-brainer! Definitely do this! Start with $50 or $500 or whatever you can. You'll be amazed how you won't miss it.

BONUS bit: Save your raise or bonus each year

Remember when I said to live like a college student? You don't have to stay on the ramen and hot dog diet, but in your first job, you will make exponentially more money than you did lifeguarding during the summer. So, you should be able to live on your salary. When you invariably get a raise or bonus, stash it in your savings and try not to change your lifestyle dramatically. Keep your meager lifestyle for a few raises and watch your savings grow.

3. Keep making those loan payments

Not a problem, you say to yourself, as if any of your lenders are kind enough to let you skip a few payments. They probably won't, nor should you skip payments. Believe it or not, at some point, you will pay off your student loan, your car loan, and your credit card balance. Take those former payments and deposit them in your savings. Call it your travel bucket, and it will make it easier to save!

AND 4. ...

You've heard of a certain type of app on your phone. Besides Candy Crush, fantasy football, and social apps, you can also find money apps to save you money. Sounds redundant, doesn't it? You can set "rules" to trigger a deposit into your savings account. Add $1.00 every time you download a song. Add $5.00 every time you reluctantly eat a meatless plant burger. That probably won't work for a carnivore like me, but if it helps you save mindlessly, then give it a go.

And Finally, Splurge Once in a While

I'm not a complete miser. You can and should take some of your savings and spend it. Travel to New Zealand. Buy an electric bike. Get crazy and order two burritos with guac and consider sharing with your roomie. Whatever puts a smile on your face and rewards you for saving, do it. Once in a while. Not too often. Rarely. Sorry, I still got a lot of dad in me.

≡GOBIT$

GOBIT #7: Start saving now. Move your savings up to the top of your budget and consider it an expense. A payment to yourself, if you will, before you pay your cell phone, credit card, or rent. If you have a job, find out if your employer offers a 401(k) or similar retirement plan. If so, enroll. If they offer a match, like 3 percent of your salary, do everything you can to at least match your company's contribution.

GOBIT #8: If you're a gig worker or have a side hustle, *absolutely* set up a business savings account in addition to your business checking account. You will need the money for expenses and taxes. Start by socking away 5 percent of what you earn. Look, you're getting paid daily in many cases, so put it away before you spend it. Divert the money automatically, and you won't miss it.

PART II:
BECOMING ADULTY

DON'T SKIP OVER THIS SECTION. I know you want to. Sure, middle school was stressful. *Where to sit in the lunchroom? Am I going to get picked for dodgeball at recess? Are there Oreos stuck in my braces? Will anybody dance with me at the mixer, or will I get shut down again?* Okay maybe these were my issues, but I'm sure you had some similar "tragic" events happen when you were twelve. They seem comical now as you look back and see how you evolved into a semi-adult. Becoming adulty means you have to start taking on some responsibility for yourself. I'm sorry. It's time!

Now, I'm not talking about crazy stuff like getting your own Netflix login or departing from your dad's cell phone plan; however, you probably do have to sign up for work benefits and your company 401(k). At some point, your mom is no longer going to make your dentist appointments for you, and you will have to go to the grocery store with some meal prep in mind. Becoming adulty is fairly self-explanatory. Don't stare at the crack in the ceiling and mumble to yourself ... we'll get through this together.

Let me start with what happens if you don't become adulty. If your mom keeps making your appointments, your dad bargains with the car mechanic, your mom manages your bank account, and your dad fills out your 401(k) paperwork for your job, then you need to grow up. Your twenties and thirties are great times to make financial mistakes, just try not to make them more than once. It's time to explore and move around and change careers and leave your parents' basement and buy your first car and maybe when you're ready, buy your first home. Trying new things allows you to make smaller mistakes and chart your own path as you age. If you don't attempt financial decisions and you let your parents, older siblings, or spouse make them all, when it's time for you to enter the game of life, you may not be ready. As an advisor, I have clients in their fifties, sixties, and seventies who had their spouse make the decisions all their lives, and then poof! they're gone. They are terrified about how to handle their money, so they hope it all works out. Don't hope. Take charge now, and you'll learn along the way.

Over the next four chapters, we'll dig into some adulty topics. Investing for the future. Having an emergency plan. Understanding your work benefits. When to change your oil. Avocado toast versus bacon and eggs. You know, important choices that will shape you for the rest of your life. So read on. That's right, just because!

My son is super. We knew early on he'd be super when he stayed an extra year for Super Kindergarten. He's continued the tradition, and now he's a Super Senior in college, and we can't wait to see the super things he'll accomplish once he finally gets through his 7 year college experience. Now he tells me he wants to get a credit card. He's pretty good with money other than cheap beer, in-game video game purchases, and fast food. Should I let him get a credit card?

Signed,

Super Hopeful Mom

Dear Super Hopeful Mom,

If his biggest spends are PBRs and Whoppers, he's probably not going to harm himself with a credit card. However, as wise adults, we know the pitfalls. Teach him that a credit card is a loan. Show him your statements. Demand it be paid off each month. It will help him build a credit history, so start him on the right path. If he can't pay cash, he shouldn't use a credit card. Share your experience with credit cards. Good luck and you might want to get the basement ready, because I'm guessing that he may be living with you for a little while.

Chapter 5
KNOW YOUR BURN

"Get control of your finances before
they get control of you!"

— Momma

BE BELOW AVERAGE

I know your mom has always said you're above average. In fact, 65 percent of us think we're above average.[3] And about 50 percent of us think we are at least average. I'm fairly decent at math, but if I type in those numbers on my nifty Casio calculator watch (precursor to smartwatch), they don't add up. I hate to break it to you, but you're not above average. Sure, Mom put your "artwork" on the fridge and collected your medals for sixth place in the three-legged race, but everyone got medals, and most of your pottery from second grade is clogging up landfills. Here's the secret ... you don't want to be average. I'm going to go out on a limb and encourage, no, beg, you to be below average! I know you're screaming, "Why didn't anyone tell me to be below average on field day in second grade? I was way below average that day!" Now's your chance to redeem yourself.

For so many reasons, don't be like the average American. We overeat, overdrink, and avoid exercise. We cry when our favorite bachelor gets booted off the island. We sweat over our fantasy football picks like we're actually running a billion-dollar sports franchise. And we don't save enough money. Why? Because it's a helluva lot more fun to whip out your debit card for the next Apple creation, a pair of trendy Lululemon jogger/yoga/pajama pants, or your winter spray tan. The fun, unlike a bad spray tan, fades pretty quickly.

So, we've already talked about mapping where you are today. What do you own and who do you owe? And then I preached to you about the glory of being a cheapskate. Channel your inner dad. And then I practically begged you to save early and often. Now that I have your attention, let's dive a little deeper into knowing your burn. How much do you spend each week? Each month? Each year? Think about it … where does your money actually go?

When I ask Kate, my college daughter, "Where does your money go?" she curls up in the fetal position and mutters incoherently to herself. To be fair, I do the same thing when my wife takes me to Bed Bath & Beyond to look at dish towels and soap dispensers. For full disclosure, Kate is amazingly thrifty with her limited college budget, and yes, I avoid any store like the plague if it doesn't have sporting equipment.

Know Your Burn
Monthly money going out

1. Food	$300
2. Rent	$1,500
3. Utilities	$200
4. Fun	$300
5. 401(k)	$1,000
6. Emergency Fund	$200
TOTAL	$3,500

It doesn't take long to put together a real-world comparison of your monthly take-home pay and your primary monthly expenses—the needs, not the wants. You need food. You want a new Toyota 4Runner. You need a place to live. You want a smartwatch. It's not hard, but as humans, we are wired to lean toward the wants. My body needs a spinach protein smoothie, but I want two Boston cream doughnuts. You see the pattern? Don't get too excited; we'll dig into what you gotta have versus what you wanna have in a few chapters.

According to the US Department of Agriculture's most recent figures, in 2021, Americans spent an average of 10.3 percent of their disposable personal income on food. Interestingly, 5.2 percent was at the grocery store and 5.1 percent was at restaurants.[4] Those numbers likely shifted once the COVID-19 pandemic took hold in 2020, but still, if you're spending around 10 percent of your budget on food, you're probably doing okay.

CASH IS SO YESTERDAY

Let's make this simple: nobody uses cash anymore. Occasionally, I scrounge up a few quarters for an afternoon half-price soda, but other than that, I have no cash on me. I'm positive if you're under forty, you have no random coins in your car's cigarette ashtray. (Do cars still have ashtrays? My cars do because my clunkers are all ten years old.) I'm going to assume you are not writing down your purchases in a notebook, on the back of a parking ticket, or on a Chipotle receipt. Nobody really writes stuff down anymore, but I assume you do have a debit card and maybe a credit card and definitely a smartphone. Look at your monthly statements! For gosh sakes, don't pitch them like they are car warranty offers.

Your statements will tell you everything you need to know. I understand you are probably not getting paper statements, but maybe you should print them out for six months for comparison. *Geez, JB, then I'd have to find a printer and paper and ughh* ... Never mind, scratch the printing idea. Download your debit and credit card statements from your bank to a PDF and save it on your secure cloud drive of choice. You don't need to do it forever, but if you do it for six months, it will force you to take a gander at your purchases. *Holy cow! I spent how much at Sushi Den, and I don't even love sushi? What the heck did I order online for $179 from Knoxville, Tennessee? Who is _____ (fill in the blank service), and why are they charging me $14.95 per month?* I've had all these conversations with myself and my kids, and it helps me to refocus (and have a family meeting about *not* spending money, which they love!) to keep an eye on things.

Step 1 is to open your statements when they arrive at your home. Step 2 is to review them. I understand that Step 1 is scary, and I'm often afraid to open the statement after a family trip (or pretty much every month), but it's time to man up. Or woman up, if that makes more sense. Download the paper statements for at least six months, and I bet you'll see some disturbing yet correctable trends in buying habits.

If you're absolutely opposed to killing trees and receiving paper, then pull up your bank app at least twice a month on Sunday nights. Pause your Bob's Burgers streamathon and take a gander at your spending. Simply looking at your online statements for fraud is one key motivation, but as a dad, I like to see what "I"/we spent on airline travel, bath soap, cell phone minutes, Uber rides, and late-night burritos.

Most credit card companies will separate your expenditures for you so you can see what categories are eating up your hard-earned funds. If you're feeling unusually nerdy, create a simple spreadsheet and compare expenses with your MoneyBuddy from back in Chapter 2 to see if you're in line or way off track.

Once you have your statements for six months, you can see where your money is "burning." Is it HBO? Doubtful, because you're still on your cousin's boyfriend's mom's account. However, maybe you are spending it on important stuff like rent, a car loan, a school loan, utilities, food, and airplane tickets. Throw in pizza, lattes, bar tabs, snakeskin boots, and in-game purchases, and you have some spending habits. I'm not saying eliminate the snakeskin boots, but don't try to disguise them as cross-trainers for working out.

Most of us remember when we bought airplane tickets to the Canary Islands. Or new powder skis for the upcoming season. It's no fun to remember every little thing, but that is where it adds up. Back in the old days ... I haven't said that for three chapters, so calm down ... I would write down my expenses because I was poor. I mean like college poor. Like mac and cheese with meat was a delicacy. I had to make sure I had enough for rent, food, and cheap beer. It was close, but I usually made it. So that's all I'm asking: keep track of your money for six months. Use a spreadsheet. A money app. Or simply eyeball your debit, credit, and Venmo accounts to see where the money went. If you need to make changes, you'll have the details right in front of you.

C'S GET DEGREES

Maybe that's not the mantra you lived by when you were in college, but certainly you saw the below-average student graduate, and now they are gainfully employed at a tech startup and crushing it. I know it's impossible to identify what is financially average these days, but as far as spending goes, aim for subpar. Don't try to keep up with the Joneses, or the Herlockers, or the Kardashians. Just be your cheap self and spend less than your friends and gloat about it! I'm not asking you to fix your spending and live like a college student, yet. I just want you to know where it's going, for now. Know your burn!

≡GOBIT$

GOBIT #9: Track your expenses … *every Sunday night*. I know you just got home from an epic powder day on the slopes, you have to meal prep for the week, you have to delete 150 emails before Monday, and, of course, FaceTime with your mom. But add "tracking expenses" to the list and check it off every Sunday. Use a money app, spreadsheet, or simple notes app on your phone. Download your debit and credit card statements for six months. Know where your money goes and why. Know your burn! If you know where it goes and why you spent it, then you can get control of your finances before they get control of you.

GOBIT #10: Take a second look at those main monthly spending categories like food, gas, and subscriptions. Subscriptions, oh my, don't get me started. Streaming services, the gym, candle of the month club? Are you really getting your money's worth? Do you even remember where that gym is? You just might find your monthly savings hiding in those careless spends.

I'm getting hassled by HR a.k.a. Human Resources. I may have put Dwight's stapler in Jell-O, or I possibly ate Phyllis's egg salad sandwich from the fridge. Nothing too criminal but HR keeps nagging me on all kinds of things, including to get ready for our OPEN ENROLLMENT next week. What exactly do I need to do to get 'ready' and do you think my colleagues will retaliate?

Signed,

Creepy Creed

Dear Creepy Creed,

Nice nickname, by the way. Dwight seems harmless, but my guess is that Phyllis will crush every bone in your body if you touch her egg salad. Open enrollment is not unlike taking a pop quiz. You can prepare by reviewing your elections from last year and deciding whether you need to make any updates. Did you sign up for disability insurance? You should. Did you participate in the 401(k)? Definitely should. Did you get married, have a kid, or get divorced? Not all in the same year, but were there any obvious significant life changes? Compare notes with colleagues in similar life stages and then go ask HR for more info. Do not rely on your cubemate to make your life decisions but instead ask HR to fill in the gaps. If you do nothing, your benefits may disappear, so don't ignore it like your mom's texts.

Chapter 6

FRIEND WITH BENNIES:
Understand Your Work Benefits

"Hey, Dad? My open enrollment is due on Monday, and I'd really rather claw my eyes out with a screwdriver and oh yah, I'm going camping this weekend. Can you make my selections for my 401(k), PPO, HSA, DI ... It's like HR has their own language. Better yet: Can I stay on your health plan?"

— My son, Jack, and every young adult

EVERY FALL, JUST LIKE HALLOWEEN and the start of another reality dating show, after Black Friday and before Cyber Monday, employers and independent health care plans throw a big party called *open enrollment*. Let me be the first to say it's an amazing experience. It's kind of like going to an outdoor concert minus the crowd, thumping music, and fun. For some reason, it seems to fly under the radar for too many of us. In fact, I've read that more than half of employees report spending more time on a haircut than on selecting their benefits.

As the owner of limited hair follicles, I proudly spend more time on my benefits enrollment versus my $9.99 special at Ray's Barber Shop & Lawn Mower Repair. In fact, I don't think I should be charged full price for my limited styling options, but that's a deeper discussion with Ray. DVR the first half of the football game (sixty minutes) and dedicate that time to review your options for medical and disability coverage, Health Savings Accounts, a 401(k), and additional benefits that will protect you from life's unexpected events and improve your financial well-being. If you don't, you may not be covered in the short term if you get sick or injured, or in the long term in retirement if you don't start socking away money into your 401(k).

I have a nephew, let's call him Tate so he doesn't tackle me next time I see him, who is wicked smart with computers, as they say in Boston. Not the sharpest tool in the shed with his personal financial life. He's made great money, since getting out of college, as a hired hacker teaching companies how to protect their computer systems. Tate could probably hack into the Sheriff's Department and erase my parking tickets if I asked him to, but he has no clue how to sign up for his 401(k) or health benefits. One weekend he went rock climbing with his buddies and slipped off a ledge and busted his leg. Not great but not terrible. Ambulance, ER, surgery, compound fracture, metal rods, and broken Ray-Bans! Most of the $25,000 in medical costs would've been covered by insurance had he remembered to sign up. He thought he was covered, but apparently, he didn't re-up with the company plan during open enrollment, and his coverage lapsed. His out-of-pocket just went from $2,500 to $25,000 because he wasn't covered. Don't suffer the same fate as Tate!

DO I HAVE YOUR ATTENTION?

Think of your open enrollment as picking your Friend with Benefits. You know that guy or gal that you kind of like once in a while but don't want to commit much effort … okay, I'm not going down that road, but you're still reading, so hang with me for another ten minutes. Your work benefits are a gift from your friend, a.k.a. employer. Don't leave them on the porch like a random package and forget to unpack them. If you are fortunate to work for an employer that provides benefits, take the time to understand them at some level.

Back when I was in my twenties (reference #7 to the author's youth), my first job gave me a huge packet with all the stuff I'd supposedly need to know before I started. It was easy. I just checked every box and sent it back. Instead of consulting HR and reading the information, I recall asking Ron in shipping over lunch what I should do. Ron was thirty years older than me with two kids, three ex-wives, and four cats, and he may have been missing his right arm, but he hid it well. Ron and I had nothing in common other than an affection for peanut butter and jelly. Consult your HR for help with benefits because you are their customer. Needless to say, I could've put forth a little more effort, but when you're in your twenties, you're invincible. Right?! What I know now is that I was probably paying too much for some of the benefits I didn't need. I didn't sign up for disability insurance because it was like twenty-five extra bucks a paycheck, which, in my twenties, converted to a couple of beers, a burger, and a few games of foosball. I thought that was outrageous. I did sign up for my 401(k), but I definitely wasn't maxing out my contributions like I should have been.

So, what should you do? Don't copy Ron's benefits or anybody ever who has four cats. Do a little homework. I'm going to try and explain the main topics in your HR packet and items to consider, but in the end, you need to spend some time researching. Yes, I'll permit you to have a frosty IPA while you fill it out if that gets you to do it. Here are a few details.

Your Company Bennies

Retirement Plan – 401(k)	Juice Bar
PTO – Paid Time Off	Life Insurance
Ongoing Training	Disability Insurance
Tuition Reimbursement	Student Loan Assistance
Health Insurance	Childcare
On-site Barista	Rail/Bus Pass

401(K): FREE MONEY!

I could give you a bunch of stats and write chapters on the pluses and minuses of company 401(k)s, but this absolutely 100 percent falls into the Sign Up and Contribute Because I Said So category. Contributions to your 401(k) are made pre-tax, which means it lowers your current income tax bill. Your employer may match your contribution (FREE MONEY) up to 3 percent or so. Don't leave that free money on the table! When investing while you're young, time is your friend—the market ups and downs actually help you with long-term upward trends. Every fifty-year-old will tell you they wish they had started investing earlier; luckily for you, your company 401(k) forces you to do it. Most companies will have a mix of funds to invest your 401(k), but they also tend to have target-date funds (more on these in Chapter 13). These target-date funds are designed to match up with your expected retirement thirty to forty years down the road. For example, if you are twenty-five years old in 2020, then you may retire in 2060 when you are sixty-five. Sounds pretty far off, but it creeps up on you. There will be target-date funds that show "TD 2060," and that is an easy choice.

Also don't leave old 401(k)s at previous jobs. Bring them with you and don't forget about them, or you may forfeit the funds. Don't overthink it. Do it. You know why!

HEALTH INSURANCE

This benefit is probably the most confusing because you never had to deal with it before. Prior to you becoming adulty, your mom would schedule your doctor's appointment for you. She would drive you to the appointment and fill out the questions in the waiting room. The doctor would use big words and then Mom would explain it in the drive-thru at Chick-fil-A, and somehow, somebody would pay the bill. Am I right? That's okay, we all did it, but now it's on you. Sign up! You're not invincible.

All the plans are a little different, but if you're young, healthy, and employed, you can probably pick the plan with a higher deductible and lower cost each month. *Deductible* means the amount you have to spend before your insurance will cover most of the cost. For example—focus for thirty seconds for me—if your deductible is $5,000, then insurance won't fully kick in until you spend $5,000 for the calendar year. If your deductible is $10,000, then your monthly insurance premium will be less because you are covering more of your insurance before you hit your deductible. Have I lost you? Are you staring at the crack in the ceiling again instead of signing up? Review your options, and if you have no underlying health issues, then it probably makes sense to sign up for the HDP (high deductible plan) with an HSA. Take a breath and finish up.

BONUS INSURANCE *BIT$* ...

Just when you thought insurance couldn't get any more exciting ... You definitely should sign up for disability insurance (a.k.a. DI) if it is offered by your company. DI will pay a portion of your wages if you can't work. Let's say you are carving up a double black diamond in Vail, and Dale from Kansas in his jeans and KC Chiefs jersey cuts you off in the middle of the ski run. You don't want to crush Dale, so you make a hard stop, catch an edge, and flip over Dale. Dale's fine, but you have a broken leg, pierced kidney, and a concussion. Sorry I had to paint a picture, but the reality is that you can't work for a while. DI protects your income in case you can't work because of injury. This type of insurance will kick in and make up for most, if not all, of your salary while you're on the shelf. VERY IMPORTANT. Sign up for it!

HSA: HEALTH SAVINGS ACCOUNT

This may or may not be offered, but HSAs are a nice perk if you have a high deductible health plan like I mentioned above. HSAs allow you to put money away pre-tax into a savings account for health care. You can use the money for dental visits, copays and acupuncture. I threw in acupuncture because HSA money sometimes can be used for healthcare that your normal plan doesn't cover. Sign up and throw in $50 to $100 per paycheck, and your employer will probably match your contributions (a.k.a. more free money) up to a point. It will add up and grow tax-free.

LIFE INSURANCE

I saved the most exciting benefit for last. If you're still reading, then I applaud you. Life insurance provides money for your loved ones in case you were to prematurely expire, a.k.a. die early. Your employer may give you 1X or 2X of your salary at no cost. That is probably sufficient until you have a mortgage, spouse, and kiddos. Once your liabilities start to increase and you have more mouths to feed, you must get more life insurance, and it would be wise to seek out a licensed professional to help with the process.

That wasn't absolutely awful, was it? This has been a short list of items to consider for open enrollment. The #1 thing is: *Don't ignore it.* Open enrollment is not a friend request on Instagram from your mom's neighbor Libby, who you can ignore. You can't stay on your parents' insurance forever, and at age twenty-six, you're going to get kicked off anyway. If and when you have questions, ask HR for help. Brooks in the cube next to you is a good dude and a decent commissioner of your fantasy team, but not an expert in your personal HR needs.

$\equiv$ GOBIT$

GOBIT #11: Contact HR about your benefits. I know Human Resources can be confusing and they throw around acronyms like PPO, HMO, HSA, and 401(k), but in reality, you are their customer. Review your current benefits on the company website and contact the department before the last day of open enrollment. Spend some time reviewing each item and what you currently have and what you should consider. Compare notes with co-workers around your age but understand that each family is unique, so your situation may be different.

GOBIT #12: Do you have a side hustle? Or maybe you're a gig worker. Lyft, Door Dash, TikTok phenom, waitress/actress/barista. Check with healthcare.gov to see what options are available. State-specific plans are ways to customize a plan that is affordable for you. Also check with your professional associations to see if they offer group coverage, which will help lower your costs. Do not ignore health coverage! At the very minimum, get what's considered catastrophic coverage with a high deductible to cover you if something major happens.

I was talking with Steve in HR, and he is squandering away his savings for an excursion to Iceland. And then Jennifer in Accounting told me that she redirects 5 percent of her paycheck into savings every period in case she needs a safety net. And finally, my dad harps on me to dump 15 percent into my 401(k) every check to save for retirement! My brain freezes, so I don't do anything. Help?

Signed,

Brain Freeze

Dear Brain Freeze,

Take a step back. I get that there are a lot of demands for your wallet, so the best plan is to have a plan. Create a rainy-day fund. Contribute to your 401(k) at least enough to get the company match. And build up your fun money for travel, a car, or a nice present for your mom! Write down your goals and then back into what you need to save. Tell a friend and keep track of each other.

Chapter 7
SH.T HAPPENS!
Build an Emergency Fund

"Create a safety net so those financial
surprises aren't surprising."

— Johnny B

HERE ARE THE TOP SEVEN "Sh.t Happens!" events that may
happen in your lifetime:

- You will back into another car in the parking lot.
- You will be late on rent because you decided to buy that
  mountain bike that you couldn't afford.
- You or your spouse will be downsized, have their posi-
  tion eliminated, get sacked, or get canned, a.k.a. get fired.
- You will take the wrong baby home from the hospital.
- Your webcam is accidentally on as you're picking your
  nose or doing something else embarrassing.
- Your furnace will go out in February during an ice storm.

* You offer to pick up the check at happy hour, and your card is declined.

Don't get the impression that I'm a Negative Natalie. A Dire Dan. A Pessimistic Pam. I'm just here to tell you about your future because I can guarantee that one, if not all, of these top seven events will happen to you in your lifetime. Yes, all but one of these happened to me. I'll let you guess which one.

There are "urgencies" and "emergencies." Urgencies mean you feel like you have to act now. Emergencies mean you will have to act now. Don't mix them up. Some events feel like emergencies because, let's face it, you dropped the ball. In reality, more sleep, better eating habits, less happy hours, consistent exercise, more veggies, less binge-watching, and saving early are all under your power. Oh wait, I was talking about all the habits I need to work on! All of us can improve, and the fact that you forgot the triple witching day of your rent, car payment, and student loan all being due on the first of the month is on you and nobody else.

SH.T ISN'T CHEAP

Real or imagined emergencies can be costly. Backing your car into a parking meter might be an emergency. Realizing your rent was due yesterday might be an emergency. Deciding that you must have a new fifty-five-inch TV for the Super Bowl would be cool but is not an emergency. (Full disclosure: I may have done this in my younger days because my team was in the big game, but I'm not advocating it since it took me three years to pay it off. I was a financial idiot. Don't be a fin-idiot.) Have an emergency fund ready for emergencies, and you won't have to dump more expenses on your high-interest credit card.

What exactly is an emergency (a.k.a. Sh.t Happens!) fund, and how much should you keep in it? The traditional rule of thumb in personal finance is that an individual or family should have three to six months of liquid assets (cash in the bank) to cover the untimely death of your refrigerator; brakes for your twenty-year-old, hand-me-down SUV; or some other unexpected event, like you got displaced, downsized, or fired. Yet according to a 2020 Bankrate survey, 56 percent of Americans don't have enough in savings to cover an unexpected expense of $1,000.[5] Twenty percent of respondents said they would put it on their credit cards, and 10 percent said they'd slink over to a family member and ask for a loan. Neither are great options, so let's set up an emergency fund.

WHAT IS NOT AN EMERGENCY FUND

Your retirement plan at work is not an emergency fund. Technically, it could be an option. Like option #25 after you've begged your stingy Aunt Robyn to part with some of her bingo winnings, swindled your niece Maeve out of her Girl Scout money, and sold off a kidney. What I'm saying is, this should be your absolute last option for an emergency. Your 401(k) or IRA is designed for retirement, so if you pull money out early (before you turn fifty-nine-and-a-half, which is the earliest you can take money out based on IRS rules), you will have to pay income taxes and a 10 percent penalty. Assume that if you withdraw $10,000 from your IRA, about $4,000 of the funds will go to the IRS to pay taxes. You have not paid taxes on your 401(k) or traditional IRA, so when you pull money out, Uncle Sam wants his cut. Avoid this option at all costs. Also, an emergency fund is not invested in crypto, real estate, or the stock market. The fund is also not tied up in your nephew's fintech startup, nor is it your open line of credit on your platinum travel credit card. It has to be readily available as cash at a moment's notice.

THE SUSPENSE IS KILLING US ... WHAT IS AN EMERGENCY FUND?

An emergency fund is a boring savings account at your bank. You're probably not earning much interest on your money, but it's there when you need it and you can pull it out today without penalty. I guess you could bury cash in a shoebox in your back-yard, but let's be adulty and use a reputable financial institution. We all know that sh.t happens, so it's nice to have a rainy-day fund to access when you crash your mountain bike, snap your collarbone, and your insurer says you need a few thousand $$ to meet your deductible. Speaking from experience, sending money to the hospital to pay the bill was unexpected and much less fun than buying a sweet new mountain bike.

Paying a few thousand for a surprise medical bill is unpleas-ant, but it is more realistic that you or your spouse could lose your job at some point, and having some reserves helps ease the pressure to accept the first new job offer to pay the bills. Keep the money in a bank of your choice, and make it easy to access.

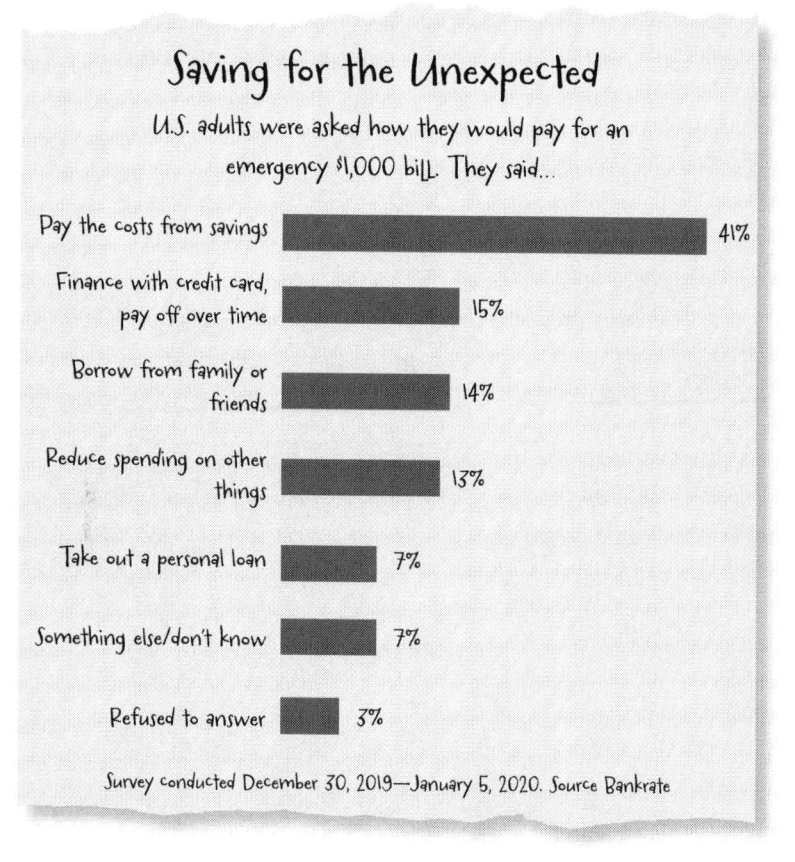

Saving for the Unexpected

U.S. adults were asked how they would pay for an emergency $1,000 bill. They said...

Pay the costs from savings	41%
Finance with credit card, pay off over time	15%
Borrow from family or friends	14%
Reduce spending on other things	13%
Take out a personal loan	7%
Something else/don't know	7%
Refused to answer	3%

Survey conducted December 30, 2019—January 5, 2020. Source Bankrate

WHERE AM I SUPPOSED TO FIND THE FUNDS?

Wow, you ask good questions! I said earlier that this pool of money should cover three to six months of expenses. These are your fixed expenses, not your variable expenses. Fixed expenses are costs you must pay—rent, food, utilities, gas, insurance, and loans, for example. If you don't pay rent, the landlord kicks you out. If you don't pay your electric bill, the power company shuts off your power and you can't charge your five devices. Variable expenses involve eating out, vacations, and your annual ski pass. Nice to have but not critical. Since we covered your burn rate back in Chapter 5, we have a rough idea of what you spend each week, each month, and throughout the year. If your fixed expenses are $3,000 per month, then you need $18,000 in an emergency fund.

$3,000 x 6 months = $18,000

I hear you thinking *Whoa, no way can I find $18,000 to hide away when I can barely cover my bus pass!* I get it, so the answer is to start with $50 per week. Or $25 or $500. Whatever you can spare to start that little side fund so when you eventually need it, you won't panic and borrow from your credit card. Bad idea! Realize that it may take years to get to your number, and then that number may increase as you add a partner and little mouths to feed. Don't fret. Just take the first step.

≡GOBIT$

GOBIT #13: Set up a savings account where you have your checking account today. I'm 98.7 percent positive you can do it all online and you won't have to go into a branch. However, the benefit of going into a branch is that you get a lollipop! Divert $50, $100, or $500 from each paycheck. When your SUV brakes eventually give out or your beloved company is eliminating your position, you won't be facing a financial emergency.

GOBIT #14: Use a calendar, whether it's on your phone, your tablet, your laptop, or the Firemen of Station 23 monthly calendar that showed up in your mailbox. Whatever helps you track your payments. Log the dates that payments are due—all of them. Don't get hit with late fees and overdraft penalties. It's a habit that might save you the equivalent of a Porsche over your lifetime.

I graduated! Yeah! They tell me I'm an adult now. Ugh! Should I pay down my student loans or contribute to my retirement plan at work? This adult stuff is hard. I liked it when my biggest decision in college was between Subway or Mickey D's.

Signed,

Should I Pay or Should I Grow

Dear Should I Pay or Should I Grow,

Congratulations on graduating. I'm sorry you have to leave your college bubble and become an adult. Your food options will improve, however. The short answer as to whether you should pay your student loans or contribute to your retirement plan is YES. As always, it depends on your specific situation, but it never hurts to start early for retirement saving. At least contribute up to the minimum needed to get your company match. And stay current with your student loans so they don't get out of control. Build a plan!

Chapter 8

GAME OF LOANS—
Paying Down Student Debt versus Investing for the Future

"Interest is coming!"

— Johnny B

CONGRATS, YOU MADE IT! Formal schooling is a few years in the rearview mirror. You're in your third job already and starting to make some real money. You're close to leaving the three smelly, loud college roomies behind. You've already accumulated a basket of old 401(k)s from previous employers, and you're not sure what to do with them. And for some unknown reason, you have a smidgen of cash left over each month after you've paid your obligations. What do you do with this newfound "wealth"? Your choices are to plan an epic hiking trip to Costa Rica, pay off your student loan, or add money to your retirement plan. Which choice should you make? Do you choose Door #1, Door #2, or Door #3? Sorry, that's an old reference to *The Price Is Right* game show that lived on daytime TV for decades. We got to watch the game show when we faked being sick to stay home from middle school. Back to the lecture ... the answer is: choose all three.

I'm not advocating blowing any extra money on exotic trips every year, but YOLO—my kids advised me to stop using "YOLO," but it's a Dad Thing now. I can't believe I'm saying this, so let's keep the YOLO on the down low from my kids, but it's healthy to splurge once in a great while. That robosavings plan we set up way back in Chapter 4 can help set you up for a reasonable vacation each year, no matter how long or short the trip might be. It could be $50 a week or $50 a month or more. Start with something and build it because it will make you smile.

WHAT'S BEHIND DOOR #2? PAYING DOWN YOUR STUDENT LOAN!

Let's hope your college friends outlast your student loan payments. Rumors circulated during the 2020 election that certain candidates would facilitate eliminating student loan debt. I wouldn't count on your government, your grandparents, or your stingy yet wealthy Uncle David to wipe out all of your student debt. It could happen, but like your dad figuring out how to take family selfies without his thumb in the picture, it's unlikely. Take ownership, make your required payments, and add a little more each month if you can. Paying more than the minimum will greatly accelerate wiping out your debt on your own.

If student debt has a good side, it is this: it usually has a low interest rate, so if you have higher debts like a car loan or credit cards, attack those first! Let me be the first to say that this is very adult-like behavior and methodical, but it will make you feel better as you chip away. Here are steps you can take now.

Who Are You Paying?

Seems straightforward, but it helps to know your service provider. Who do you pay? When is your payment due? What is the minimum you must pay each month? What is your interest rate?

Consider Consolidating Your Student Loans

If you have multiple loans, you may be able to combine them to lower your interest rate. **However**, don't automatically consolidate your private loans with your loans backed by the federal government. "That is so interesting; please tell me more," you ask sarcastically? Let's say you have three student loans with different interest rates because of when you initially received the funds. For example:

Game of Loans

Loan #1
$12,000 at 4 percent interest rate from
Discover Bank – December 2016

Loan #2
$16,000 at 3.5 percent interest rate from Sallie Mae
(backed by the Federal Government) – January 2018

Loan #3
$8,000 at 3.75 percent interest rate from
Sallie Mae – December 2019

If you have three student loans, you may have different interest rates. One may be a private loan from a bank, and the others may be backed by the federal government. Keep the lowest-rate loans if they are cheaper than the current rates. And if, by chance, you need to defer some of your payments because of a job loss, your federal loans may be deferred but a private loan from a bank probably cannot because that is up to each financial institution. Deferral of payments is not the elimination of payments, so don't forget about them when they come due again. Before you decide to consolidate, talk it over with your MoneyBuddy, Dad, or a financial advisor to get a second opinion.

Review Your Payment Options

You may be able to pay more each month or defer paying if you go back to grad school or lose your job. It's possible that your payments could be eliminated if you work for a qualifying public institution for a period of ten years or more. Again, do your research and don't let advertisers sway you. Companies that text, email, and call you constantly want you to consolidate your loans and are in business to make money. They are not your buddies! Don't hesitate to ask a trusted friend or family member who has a good financial background to see what they would recommend you do.

Time is on your side with investing, so don't squander it.

And last but not least, behind Door #3 is investing for the future. "Don't squander it" is kind of harsh, but if I just wrote that retirement is coming, you wouldn't read anymore. Retirement may be so far off that you feel you can put it off like going to the gym. It is decades away, but you must start early!

By the way, this advice isn't meant to be in the order of one, then two, then three. It's one, two, and three. Start by at least putting in the minimum to get your company match for your 401(k). If they match your first 3 percent, then put in 3 percent. If they put in another 50 percent of your 3 percent contribution, then try to do that too. Once you start diverting more money to your retirement, you won't miss it. Increase it 1 percent each year religiously, and you should be ecstatic with your balance in thirty years.

The Game of Student Loans is not quite as fun as Yahtzee, but it is controllable. Here are a few ideas to get you started in managing your student debt.

≡GOBIT$

GOBIT #15: Open up your calendar app and add dates when your student loan payments are due each month. Make the minimum payment. Research with your loan provider how long before you will have it paid off. If you can pay more each month, this could dramatically lower the lifetime cost of your loan. Do you have multiple student loans? Consider consolidating your loans if it lowers your interest rate, but be very careful if you have government-backed loans. Even if a private bank has better rates, the government loan may have additional benefits of forbearance or partial forgiveness that private loans can't offer. Do your homework and get advice if you need answers.

GOBIT #16: I convinced you to contribute to your 401(k), so let's plan on increasing your amount by 1 percent each year. Your company plan will probably allow you to do this automatically, so take advantage of it. Don't think. Do. Assuming you get a raise or bonus each year, put that toward savings. At least make the minimum contribution to your 401(k) to get your company match. This is free money from your employer, so you want to at least get started. If you can max out your contribution, then definitely make the effort. Your future self will thank you.

PART III: GET YOURS

FORGET EVERYTHING YOUR MOM TAUGHT you about sharing when you were a toddler. Blasphemy! Of course, I'm coming at you from a dad's point of view, but throwing out all the good stuff that Mom taught us? I'm not saying stop washing your hands or forgo the bike helmet, but this is where I encourage you to go get yours. We're halfway through, and all I've preached to you is to save and not spend and be adulty, and I wouldn't be surprised if you already chucked this book out of your car window on your way to the Saturday farmers market. Yes, you need to be thrifty if you want to get through life, but it helps to have goals. I will continue to beg you to save for retirement, but

I understand that it is so far off that you need some near-term goals.

Let's start with a few simple items that you want. Go ahead and get that Reese's chocolate at the checkout counter. I'll allow it. Every so often, I'll permit you to get the latest tech gadget to add to your collection. If, and a big IF, you are being a good finbitter (saving regularly, spending wisely, and questioning every purchase), then you need to reward yourself. Small things that you wouldn't normally buy are permitted. I can't believe I'm allowing you to spend money, but I'm not completely cruel. Maybe you've saved up for that new pair of sandals—the ones you could've bought as the off-brand at Walmart, but you want the name brand from Gucci. Find a sale and get them! Don't buy that new golf driver in June but buy it in January when it's on sale. Reward yourself smartly.

Let's say you're really on the financial ball and you want to trade in the minivan hand-me-down from Mom that you've been driving since high school. You want an adult set of wheels with a stereo from this century. It's okay to plan for it and get the right vehicle for you. Maybe you're good with riding the light rail to work and having your friends cart you around to the grocery store and hiking trails. You don't want a car, but you do want to start checking off countries around the world to visit. Buying a car seems like a hassle to you but planning a trip to Taiwan, Myanmar, and Vietnam is right up your alley. Go for it!

If you really want to put on your big girl pants, it's time to buy that condo in the city. You love your roomies, but you're dying to have your own bathroom and not have to watch *Squid Game* when you really want to watch *Sunday Night Football*. Owning your home is a big step in adulthood, and some may take years to get there. Getting your stuff takes planning and saving and blah blah blah, but it will allow you to continue to move toward full-fledged adulting. So read on. That's right ... you know what I'm going to say!

I was wrastlin' with my GrandPapa Den over the last piece of pumpkin pie at Thanksgiving, and he pulled the old "I only have so many years left on this planet, and I really need it for my glaucoma." I don't see the connection with glaucoma, but I guess I've got a few more years ahead of me. As he was inhaling his third piece of pie, he went on to tell me I should quit buying all of this junk like computers, cell phone cases, and leather pants. He insisted I should pay my bills every month and only buy what I really need. Can you translate what that pie thief was trying to say to me?

Signed,

Pumpkin Pie-less Peyton

Dear Pumpkin Pie-less Peyton,

If Papa Den wants the last piece of pie, Papa Den gets the last piece of pie. No wrastlin' required. Not sure of the medical connection, but he gets a little latitude at his age. In many ways, he didn't have a lot of purchasing options as he was entering adulthood, so it kills him to see his lineage waste money on leather pants and lattes. Try not to be too frivolous with your funds, and when Papa Den is staying at your home, make him a crappy cup of instant coffee, and he'll be so proud!

Chapter 9

AWESOME STUFF YOU WANT VERSUS BORING STUFF YOU NEED

"I love money. I love everything about it. I bought
some pretty good stuff. Got me a $300 pair of
socks. Got a fur sink. An electric dog polisher.
A gasoline-powered turtleneck sweater. And,
of course, I bought some dumb stuff, too."

— Steve Martin (comedian and actor)

"DO I NEED IT?" is the title of a lesson plan in some kindergarten classrooms. I kid you not! Along with Finger Painting and
Advanced Nose-Picking, "wants versus needs" is a lesson we
apparently need to learn in our formative years. Some brainiacs
thought that early in life, we should know the difference between
what we want versus what we need because it could help shape
our buying habits for decades to come. Wow, I must've been

drooling on my desk when Sister Jane Albert was covering that lesson. Even the occasional ruler smack to the back of my head didn't zap my attention back to whatever was being taught.

Fortunately for my finances, despite sleeping through kindergarten, I'm okay not spending money. In fact, occasionally I get physically ill when my family spends money. I'm a natural cheapskate, as I may have mentioned a few chapters ago. But for some, it's a far bigger challenge to avoid blowing money …

Americans make up to 156 impulse purchases every year, spending up to $5,400 annually, or $324,000 over their lifetime.[6]

M&Ms, swimsuits, soap dishes, concert tickets, iPads, rounds of shots for the whole bar, boots, golf clubs, plane tickets, bubble gum, and a puppy may have all been impulsively purchased by someone under my roof. Personally, I think 156 impulse buys is a little low.

Technically, it's not your fault. You have a behavior flaw. Don't take it personally; I mean the plural "you" like all of us.

We think we are rational beings and will always make the right decisions at the right times. It's easy to spend money and a lot harder to save it. That's a fact. I'm sure I could dig up a cool data point, but just think about your habits. Do you want to book a nature exploration to Yellowstone or save for retirement in forty years? Now, we make many of our purchases from the comfort of our couches. Back when I was younger (dad reference #23), we had to physically hoof it to the store, uphill, both ways, with the scorching humidity piercing every pore of our bodies (too much?), walk aimlessly around the store, and then literally give our cash to another human. It took a fair amount of effort to spend money. The physical act of handing the cashier money is the last chance to bail on a dumb purchase.

ONE OF MY NEAR MISSES ...

Do I really need this Alpine stereo for my 1974 Fiat convertible? Yes, that was my first car, and yes, I almost bought the stereo. However, when I was handing the car stereo dude my hard-earned cash, I got cold feet. I quickly realized the stereo would be worth twice as much as my crappy car, so I turned and bolted out of the store like a toddler running away from his mom.

Today, when you have a moment of rational sanity and pause your purchase while shopping online, what happens next? You get an email that says you left something in your shopping cart. And then pop-up ads track every site you're on like a corner drug dealer pushing meth on you. And then you get more emails. And then you forget why you were going to buy the item in the first place. And then you get angry at the pop-ups! Okay, I'm done with that rant. It's fine to delete the targeted emails and then unsubscribe and then just plain avoid the online pushers in order to focus on acquiring things you truly need.

KATCHING UP WITH THE KINDERGARTNERS

When you were five, you wanted the Chocolate Kazoo Spinaroo Sugar Cereal, and you relentlessly hounded your mom to add it to the grocery cart. As an adult, you want a gluten-free cinnamon roll with dairy-free frosting that doesn't taste like a pizza box. We haven't changed that much, but our wants have gotten a little more sophisticated, and now we have to cover the cost. How do you decide if something, especially something that will really bend your debit card, is a "need" or a "want"?

I can feel you rolling your eyes at me. *But JB, you've covered being a cheapskate in Chapter 3.* Yes, but this is different. Obviously, we as humans still have behavioral deficiencies that cause us to buy robotic vacuums at 2:00 a.m. or pay thousands more for the glacier blue exterior for our SUV, or casually pay $5 to grab the in-game purchase of a BFG 9000 Gravity Gun as you battle alien zombies with your video game buddies around the country.

So, one simple dorky way to prioritize and manage your finances is to categorize where you spend money into "needs" and "wants." Earlier in Chapter 3, I shamed you into being cheap. To simplify, you must start with the "needs" list. Let's start with a real survival list like you were going camping. Not baby-boomer camping in a thirty-foot, self-contained RV with AC and satellite TV, but hike-in-five-miles camping with just what you can carry so you don't have to lug it ten miles roundtrip. (Note: 5 multiplied by 2 = 10.)

WANTS VERSUS NEEDS

Food* and water are staples—if you were camping, you wouldn't carry in sushi, crab legs, and coconut water. Probably PB&Js, trail mix, and tap water. A handful of needs are easy to identify: rent, water, food,* electricity, car, gas, phone, and insurance.

Then the hard part kicks in. Do you need internet service? Probably, especially if you are lucky enough to work remotely some days. Do you need subscriptions to Spotify, Netflix, Hulu Plus, Xbox Live, and HBO? Especially now that Dad has booted you from the family plan(s)? Nope. Do you need a car? Unless you live and work in a big city with reliable public transportation, that's probably a need. Do you need an $800 monthly car payment for a sweet Jeep Cherokee 4x4? Nope—that 2011 Honda Civic with four decent tires and a little rust will do.

BUT I WANT IT NOW!

I can imagine you pouting and stomping your feet. I know this sounds redundant, but I want—no, need—to pound it into your reptilian brain. The part of your brain that is wired for survival, including breathing. Do you have to eliminate all wants from your life? Not completely and not forever, but you do have to demonstrate some discipline, dammit! If you have money in your monthly budget after covering the cost of your needs, congratulations. But don't get cocky. Is there anything left? Um, no, four bucks is not a lot, but that remainder is what you can now allocate to your "wants." Designer phone cases, pedicures, acai bowls, and Xbox games, for instance.

I'll come clean with you. Wants versus Needs is a challenge for everybody. But if you can pinpoint what you truly need, you'll be able to buy an occasional Want. You'll start to see a trend if you rewire your brain when it comes to buying stuff. Some of you may never achieve cheapskate status, but if you can at least question every purchase, you're way ahead of most other humans. Once you start to question your purchases, you'll see all the dumb stuff other people buy. Soon you'll start to make snide comments when your boyfriend decides to buy another video game. (Side note: If your boyfriend or hubby is still buying video games and you don't have kids, then you may want to exchange him for an upgrade. Back to judging others ...) When you see all the dumb stuff people buy, then you'll easily be able to reassess your own spending habits. Once you're a parent, you really get to exert your non-purchasing power, and that feels awesome, let me tell you!

All right, here are two **GOBIT$** to get you rolling ...

=GOBIT$

GOBIT #17: Make a legitimate "needs versus wants" list. This is a three-minute exercise. It's less time than it takes to floss your teeth. (You are flossing, right?) Draw a line across the top of the page, and then draw one down the middle so you have a big "T." Be honest and write down the needs on one side and the wants on the other. Send it to your dad for final analysis. I'm serious. He'll be happy to deliver a big ole dose of dad wisdom.

GOBIT #18: Need a little more motivation? Set aside some of your Want money each month to save for a purchase that feels a little extravagant—like tickets to an NHL game or a spa day. If you're doing this right, you might be able to pull off these little celebrations every few months. I'm not a complete jerk. You need to have a little fun. Once in a while. Not too often. Rarely.

* The "food" category is ripe for abuse. Do you need food to survive? Of course. Do you need to eat sushi five times a week? Nope. Like it or not, dining out (yes, this includes takeout and drive-thru) does not meet the food "Need" test.

Hey JB?

My roommate Sparky is a good dude. Sure he is twenty-nine, lives on my couch, is on his eleventh gap year before college, is not currently seeking employment, and smells something awful, but he used to be a valedictorian in pre-K. I think he can get back to his previous heights. He's a really thrifty traveler. Like he knows how to find family, friends, and recent acquaintances to bunk with as he bounces around the country. He says he can teach me the ways of couch surfing, but I've got that remote job and girlfriend and not a lot of extra travel time. Also I need to get my couch back so I can focus on my fantasy football team and improving my *Call of Duty* ranking. Any ideas on whether I should hold on to my old pal or fold up the sofa sleeper on him?

Signed,

Should I Hold Him or Fold Him?

Dear Should I Hold Him or Fold Him,

Sometimes you walk away and sometimes you run. Sparky needs to go. I read your question five times to see if there was any reason to keep him, and I got nothing. Maybe you can trick him into making a budget, and he'll leave on his own. Stick with me for a second. Tell him you want the two of you to backpack across South Asia for a month. Could he take the reins and plan it all out? Map out the places to go, plane tickets, hostels, food, and excursions? Hypothetically, he gets excited and builds a spreadsheet and analyzes the costs and actually buys a map. At some point, he may realize he has no money and he needs to get his act together. Maybe he assembles an unbelievable itinerary in a reasonable budget. Or maybe you change the door locks next time he Ubers to Dunkin'.

Chapter 10

GO TRAVEL THE WORLD

"Create a life that people assume you're living based on your social posts."

— Johnny B

LET'S FACE IT: YOU DIDN'T GO TO SCHOOL for sixteen years to sit in a cubicle. It's time to get out and see the world. In a study by Airbnb, Millennials put travel above buying a home or paying down debt. Even saving money for retirement was in a dead heat with traveling the world.[7]

Back when I was your age (here we go again...), I wanted to buy a house. My Gen Z/Millennial kids want to travel. As a dad, believe it or not, I agree with my kids.

Go travel the world! What's the catch? It's now or never. Okay, it's not that dire, but you should do it, dare I say, you need to do it, while you're young because before you know it, you'll have a mortgage, a faulty car transmission, a dishwasher leak, little hungry humans tugging at your leg, and random subscriptions to unknown services. That's just every dad's reality, but it does creep up on you. I'm not advocating you spend a romantic weekend with Juan Carlos in Barcelona, but you should go see the world. What should you do first?

My bet is that if you consider yourself the worst planner in the world and you think you are horrible with money, then you'll be able to pull together an awesome trip to Belize with your gal pals or a Vegas golf weekbender with your fellow bros for a bargain if you so desire. Why is that? Why can you rack up credit card debt and have late fees on your rent, but planning a trip with your buds is second nature? Why? Because it will be an experience like no other and you must coordinate work, flights, hotel, and friends' schedules. You know it will be fun (unless Katie has too many margs and disappears with the snorkel guide again, and you have to convene a search party on Sunday before your flight leaves). Backpacking, family excursions, Vegas golf trips, or a Nashville weekend will all create memories, and nothing happens until you start planning. Most of the time, you can't just pack a duffel bag and start walking; you'll need a little advance notice.

MAKING PLANS

#1: Find a travel buddy

This is easy, right? Who doesn't want to go somewhere at some point with some buddy? Find somebody or some group that will share the load of organizing the trip of a lifetime. If you ask Owen and he says that's awesome, let me know when we leave, then he is probably not the travel buddy you want on the front end. Pick Eli! He is fun and organized and will follow through—you know, "that" friend!

#2: Start the research

Initially this is the fun part because the world is wide open. Are you going backpacking for a week, a month, or six months?

Are you starting to piece together why we did the exercises in the previous chapters?

* Where are you today?
* Find a MoneyBuddy.
* How much money do you now have in savings? Not much. That's okay.
* How much $$$ do you make? Take out taxes. That's respectable.
* Now for the tough question. Know your burn! How much do you spend?
* What's left over? Rut-Ro! Not much.

How much will this excursion cost? No clue, but more than you're hoarding in your Venmo account. Will it be worth it? Life-changing! How much do you have to save each week to make it happen? *Wait, what?* Am I tricking you into making a BUDGET?

You got me. I know you don't want to make a budget, track your expenses, and feel guilty for buying that sweet sixty-five-inch television for gaming, but unless you hit the lottery (and you won't), this is your best path to creating a travel fund. Don't think of it as a budget. Think of it as your next chapter before full-on adulting begins, a way to experience new cultures, eat weird food, and lose track of time. If I had used the "B" word at the beginning of this chapter, I know you'd skip right over. I would. Budgeting sucks. There, I said it loud and proud. However, I've found that when I have a destination for my budget, I can stay on track.

TRAVEL FUNDS

You can create a travel fund (a.k.a. budget) in several ways. The key is to find the system that works for you. I know a TINK (two income no kids) couple—Aubrey and Ally—that writes down every expense on a pad of paper, has a cash allowance for each week, and generally seems miserable. They make great money and are on track to retire early, but Aubrey has Ally on financial lockdown, and they just seem a little tense about money. However, it works for them, or at least for Aubrey, and it's better than hoping you have money in your travel fund after a few years.

If writing down everything helps, I suggest you do it, but I'm guessing it will be hard to stick to that plan every week. Luckily, this little internet thing that Al Gore invented has allowed us to create budgets in a more systematic fashion. (To be fair, former vice president Gore never said he "invented" the internet. Rather, he said he took the initiative in "creating" the internet. Tomato, tom-ahhto!) Anyway, with your credit and debit cards, you can now view all your purchases online. I doubt you are using much cash these days, so if you are using your plastic card(s) wisely, then you can get a monthly view of where your money is going like I brought up back in Chapter 5 about knowing your burn.

Your credit card will automatically categorize each purchase. Food, entertainment, travel, utilities, and clothing are some of the spending categories. Most major bank credit cards also have budgeting software included with your credit card services. They like you and want you to use their card, so they will try and keep you on their website.

If you want to get really nerdy, then you can compare your spending categories to those of other humans. For example, your credit card may say you spend 75 percent of your monthly total on clothing. Seems like you are buying a lot of shoes. Or it may say that you spend 53 percent of your monthly total on entertainment. That is a lot of avocado toast/bottomless mimosa brunches, indie band concerts, sports betting, and axe-throwing competitions. I'm not here to judge your entertainment; I'm here to help you see where your money goes.

Budget Spreadsheet

TOTAL Income	
TOTAL Expenses	
Available to Budget	

Savings Goals	Budgeted
Emergency Savings	
Short-Term Savings Goal	
Long-Term Savings Goal	
Retirement Account	
Other	
Occasional Expenses	
Total Savings Goals	

Income	Budgeted
Income 1	
Income 2	
Income 3	
Other	
Other	
Total Income	

Debt Payments	
Mortgage	
Student Loan	
Auto Loan	
Credit Card	
Other	
Other	
Other	

Variable Living Costs	
Groceries	
Fast Food	
Gas for Car	
Ride-Sharing Services, Tolls, and Parking	
Clothes	
Dry Cleaning	
Exercise / Gym	

MAKE IT HAPPEN

Fine, JB, you tricked me into creating a travel fund budget. How do I start?

This is the perfect time to ask that question because when it comes to our progress through this book, *Whoa, we're halfway there!* If you've followed the steps so far in this book, then you've already defined what you make, what you have, and what you spend. Now you're ready to print pictures of your future world tour and plaster them to your bathroom mirror or on your bedroom ceiling. Someplace where you'll see them every day. Research, research, ask buddies, and then research some more what it will cost. Don't sandbag the cost! Which means don't underestimate the flights, the hotels, the food, the drinks, the camel rides, the bungee jumping or the hiking shoes. Let's say you'll need $25,000 to travel the world for a year. Might be high but might be low. Now you have a target, and you can start to add to the fund each week. When you analyze your spending versus your buddy's spending, maybe you notice that she spends a boatload on entertainment, but you go over on clothes. Try to whittle down each category and then stick to it. Use a popular money app to keep track or just enter it in a spreadsheet.

Once your spending habits or non-spending habits become like flossing your teeth (we discussed flossing already), it will be easier to stick to your budget. You will stray once in a while, but who doesn't have a cheat day and eat a double cheeseburger and chili fries during a diet every so often? The key is to get back to that spin class. Is that too many metaphors? You know what I mean. Check in with your MoneyBuddy and try to stick to your budget and grow that travel fund.

Finally, don't get discouraged if your GO TRAVEL THE WORLD glass jar on the counter is slow to grow. Commit to a plan, and then start dreaming of Paris, or Thailand, or Branson (if that's your sort of thing). Take little excursions as your budget is working to reward yourself. Before you know it, you'll be belly-flopping off a cliff in Dubrovnik, Croatia.

⟩⟩⟩**GOBIT$**

GOBIT #19: Pick a region you want to travel. Estimate how long you'll travel. Research the costs. Start a spreadsheet or find an app. Flights to/from and between destinations. Lodging including hostels, motels, park benches, and distant relatives! Food budget per day. Excursions like bungee jumping, camel rides, or snorkeling with humpback whales. Gear including hiking boots, backpack, and outerwear for inclement weather. You can research what you need for where you're going. Don't underestimate your expenses. Which means add up everything and then add 25 percent to the total. If you budget $10,000 for this trip of a lifetime, then add 25 percent or $2,500 just to be sure. And finally, have a backup credit card if/when things go sideways on your journey. Who are we kidding? This is the fun stuff!

GOBIT #20: Buy a *big* world map. For gosh sakes, draw the continents on a blank wall in your home even if you have zero artistic talent. Dream and plan for travel years in advance. Drop a pin of where you've been and where you want to go. Ask your friends about their best and worst destinations. Some studies show that dreaming about travel is better than actually traveling. I disagree wholeheartedly; however, it does help to focus your day job on what is important to you and your family.

I'm thinking of saving the world. I'm not sure how just yet, but I've got a few ideas. In the process, I've traded in my gas-guzzling, hand-me-down Suburban for an eBike. Probably get a Tesla, you know, because it's good for the environment and it's pretty cool. I mean, can you imagine my Tesla driving me to my spin class; I never touch the steering wheel. Whoa! I'm getting excited. Anyhoo, do you think a Tesla is a good investment in addition to making the world a better place?

Signed,

Karbonfree Karly

Dear Karbonfree Karly,

Thank you for carbon offsetting those rednecks with Ford F150 pickups who carelessly drive around with their AC on and windows down on their way to JimBob's BBQ and Bait Shop! Is a Tesla car a good investment? NO. Is a VW Bus a promising investment? NO. Should you consider any car an investment? No. Cars are what we call *depreciating assets*. As soon as you drive it off the lot or have it delivered on a flatbed via some car website, it loses value. Maybe you discover a vintage 1966 Mustang convertible hidden in Grandpa's garage, but I'd just consider a car as a form of transportation. Have a reasonable, non-emotional human like your dad help you buy a car. He loves haggling, and he may just talk you out of that next-gen car for a nice, reliable efficient commuter.

Chapter 11

I WANT MY VERY OWN COOL CAR

"I want a car that looks like a Jeep, drives like a
Porsche, has tech like a Tesla, gets gas mileage
like a Prius, and costs as little as a used bicycle."

— Johnny B

"**C'MON DOWN TO ROCKY'S AUTO EMPORIUM.** We've
got SUVs, convertibles, trucks, station wagons, electric vehicles,
hybrids, and fun four-wheelers. Our exclusive no-haggle pricing
means we have one great price for you! We have over ten acres
of low mileage, gently used creampuffs. Hurry down before we
sell your next car to someone else!"

Maybe I exaggerated a little, but you know the above
car promo is not far off. Seriously, if you don't want to SAVE
THOUSANDS and you feel comfortable overpaying on your next
car purchase, then skip this chapter. Hmm, now I've got your
attention?

Car buying has evolved quite a bit over the years. Apparently, now you don't have to leave your hammock to search for and buy a car.

Let's see, I'll go to the vending machine and get some Skittles, a can of Pringles, and that red Mustang with leather seats and chrome wheels.

Alibaba, a behemoth Chinese e-commerce company, is changing the game again and has entered the car market in China. A customer can research cars, schedule a test drive, negotiate the price, and buy the car without ever being stalked in a car lot. Sounds kind of boring to me, but I think it will be appealing to many consumers. The idea of a vending machine dispensing your car may be amusing for the good ole USA, but apparently it's very effective in China.

The Chinese consumer has embraced buying almost everything online, including cars. I don't think the US car-purchasing process is too far behind. A car vending machine has been built off the highway in Denver, Colorado. Sad to say, those ridiculously large balloon stick figures at car lots might become a thing of the past if you can make the entire purchase online. Actually, I feel sorry for you as a first-time car-buying consumer. I believe your generation is going to miss one of the true steppingstones of becoming an adult ... literally walking on a car dealer lot to look for a car. "Larry" is wearing a short-sleeve shirt with mustard-color pit stains and a tie that goes halfway to his waist. His pants are just a little too short and a little too tight. His comb-over reveals his refusal to accept his balding dome, and his yellowed teeth reveal his refusal to brush daily, especially after coffee. Other than that, he's a great guy to talk to unless you had other plans for the afternoon. As you try to read the car sticker, you feel his presence lurking nearby. If Larry made a direct route to you from the showroom and you saw him coming, you'd run. But since he weaves in and out of the parked cars like he's returning a kickoff, you're not sure if he's coming in your direction or not. He's good. Not great, but good.

Larry, a.k.a. Used Car Sales Guy: "So tell me, young lady, what brought you onto my lot today?"

Kendall, muttering to herself: "Dangnabit, he found me."

Kendall: "I'm bored, and I wanted to talk to someone, so I came to a car lot."

Used Car Sales Guy: "C'mon now, tell me how much you want to spend each month, and I'll put you in the car of your dreams!"

Kendall: "I'm just browsing. And I was excited to test drive this SUV until you snuck up on me."

Now she must figure out her exit plan. *Nuclear warheads incoming. Next season of* Stranger Things *starts tonight. Time to organize my personal finances, haha. I've decided to save the world, reduce my carbon footprint, and walk everywhere.*

It's too bad that most youngsters may never get the chance to haggle with Larry. I'm one of the few humans who enjoyed the experience. It was a game to get the car I wanted at the cheapest price with bonus free car mats. I always won because I could walk away from a deal. On several occasions, I was told by the general manager at a car dealership that I was wasting "his" time and to never step foot on their lot again! And then he reluctantly sold me the car I wanted at the price I wanted. Winner, winner, chicken dinner! Sadly, that enlightening experience, the delight of only a few deranged dads, is disappearing.

I'd like to say that I have always completed a thorough research project before buying a car, but occasionally I got a little excited and pulled the trigger too fast. My first car that I bought at age sixteen was a bright orange Fiat convertible. Looked cool. Sounded awesome. Piece of crap! Even my dad, who knows zilch, notta, zip about cars, said at the time, "Johnny, you don't want to buy this money pit." Well, at sixteen years old, you do the exact opposite to show the old man how wrong he is. My dad could have given me countless reasons not to buy the old Italian convertible, but a blatant "Because I said so!" would have sufficed. It was my money, so he let me buy it, and it was the best lesson I ever learned.

This is how I remember my first convertible ...

But this picture shows the reality most of the time.

It rarely ran, and I could've rented a convertible for two years and saved countless trips to Vito's Italian Auto Repair. Since that emotional purchase, almost all of my cars have been reliable. Buying a car is exciting, scary, and expensive, and it used to be time-consuming. Now, research is easy and you can have your car delivered within days. Buckle up! Let's go through the car-buying process in the 2020s.

FUNCTIONAL VERSUS FLASHY

Ask yourself or have an objective person not named Larry interrogate you about what you are looking for in a car.

Do you need an SUV to go off-roading in Moab as you look for the ideal hiking trail, or do you need an efficient hybrid for commuting?

Are you thinking of a sweet new ride with an epic Granite Crystal Metallic paint scheme, or will any gray do?

How much can you spend annually on gas, maintenance, repairs, and parking?

How long do you plan on owning this car?

Have you considered leasing a car like a long-term rental?

How many miles will you drive each year?

Maybe you don't have all the answers, but at least you will think about them. Next ...

Once you narrow down the type of car you want, then steer your way in the direction of two research websites. Kelley Blue Book (kbb.com) is a great tool to double-check the price of the car you are considering. You can search for other cars that are similar both locally and around the country. It's a great way to see if you're getting a good deal and if you should search further for a great deal. Always strive for the GREAT DEAL! Also scroll over to carcomplaints.com prior to signing the contract. This is kind of nerdy, but the site aggregates various sources about crash safety, recall notices, and tech service bulletins from the Insurance Institute for Highway Safety (IIHS) and the National Highway Traffic Safety Administration. As much as you may love your matte black pickup, you want to make certain that it doesn't have a costly repair record.

My personal preference is to buy a car that has come off a three-year lease. Why? The car will have low miles and maybe some warranty left, and it costs considerably less money than buying a new one. The previous driver had to take good care of the vehicle to get their deposit back, so you can expect it to be in good shape. The car may not be the perfect color, but to save thousands, it may be worth it.

Here are two additional research sites to consider once you have settled on the ideal car: edmunds.com and carfax.com. Both sites allow you to compare vehicles of the same year and similar mileage. This will give you some negotiating knowledge with the seller when you really lock in on that ideal set of wheels.

Finally, you've found the absolutely perfect vehicle.

Fire-engine red with black leather. It has low miles and is the right price. The critical next step is to have an independent mechanic pop the hood and give the vehicle a full inspection. This may cost you $75 to $150. It's worth every penny and could save you thousands. Walk away from a deal that is not ideal for you. You want this SUV, but you don't need this SUV. There will be other SUVs, so forget about this one if it isn't the best choice.

And finally, don't be afraid to haggle. I demand you haggle. Since most of the haggling is online now or via text, it never hurts to throw out a lower price. Don't believe it when they say they have a no-haggle price! Haggle like a middle-schooler wanting more time for gaming! If you save a couple hundred bucks, it's a victory. If it terrifies you to negotiate, then bring in a stunt haggler. A DAD! For all the times Dad embarrassed the family with his cheapness, like limiting the drinks to tap water at Applebee's, at this moment, you want him to bring out his world-class frugality. Let Dad ride shotgun on your negotiating as you operate the haggle-texting with the sales guy or chatbot or whoever is on the other side. You operate the texting with the dealer, and Dad will be in your corner to keep you from caving in. Dad was born for this, and he will be thrilled to be called in off the bench to assist.

SHOW THEM THE MONEY

Everything checks out, and now it's time to figure out how to pay for the truck/SUV/convertible/electric vehicle/hybrid of your dreams. Do you buy it with cash? Should you lease it? Should you finance it through the dealer? Should you borrow from Mom and Pop? Do you contact your bank or credit union to check their rates?

Yes! Just like finding the perfect ride, you want to explore all your financing options. Some say you should do this prior to finding the dream car, but I think you can research the car and finances simultaneously. Seriously, looking for a car is a helluva lot more fun than figuring out how to pay for it. But eventually, you'll have to solve that financing conundrum, so let's cruise through your options.

- Cash: Easy but may not be an option in your early years. A combo of cash and low-rate financing may be option #1.
- Parents, father-in-law, big brother: I've borrowed from all these family members back in my twenties, and it worked out okay, but I'd rather not owe family. Thanksgiving gets weird with your father-in-law when you're late on a payment. If it isn't too awkward, then don't rule it out.
- Finance through a car dealer, bank, or credit union: It really doesn't matter. Again, I've used all three in my past. Go with whoever will give you the best terms: the lowest interest rate, fewest years of loan, and smallest down payment. You're not trying to make friends; you're trying to get the best deal. If this car math isn't your thing, recruit one of your nerdy buddies or your old man to look at your options. Surely you know someone who can whip up a spreadsheet and explore the best deal. You'll owe them a margarita and some street tacos, which is money well spent.
- Leasing the vehicle: A lease is a three-year rental with a hefty down payment. Dealers push leases because they know you want the newest car and they make the most

profit. If you want a new car under warranty every three years, consider a lease. I've never leased a car because I thought it was too expensive and I didn't want to be limited in the miles I could drive. Leasing can be a good option for business use because you may be able to write it off as an expense, but the arrangement usually favors the dealer. In my biased Dad opinion, don't lease! But as I mentioned earlier, try to buy a car that just came off a lease because it is probably in pretty good shape and costs thousands less than a new car.

Do you feel you have enough car knowledge to find your dream four-by-four or efficient commuter EV sedan? Knowledge is power, and the more you know about the car-buying process, the better off you'll be.

≡GOBIT$

GOBIT #21: Before you start test-driving Teslas, do your homework. Find the right type of car for your needs and then narrow down your search. Plan out the approximate costs in a spreadsheet or app before you jump in. Consider your payment, insurance, maintenance, gas, and major repairs. Edmunds.com is a good place to calculate the cost of car ownership. The more you research, the more money you'll save.

GOBIT #22: Let's talk about car insurance. Unless you've been living in a van down by the river with no Wi-Fi, I have no doubt that you can name five car insurance companies that will let you bundle your auto and home insurance! Annoying ads, but actually a good idea if you can do it. Shop around. Understand the line items in the quote and go with the best price. You can always change companies, and they will refund what you've paid to the current day. If you pay annually, you'll get a discount, but starting out monthly may make your cash flow smoother. Do your homework and compare notes with your family and friends. Ask Dad who he uses, and I bet you can teach him a thing or two about saving money on insurance. He may tear up a bit because he'll be so proud.

I think I need to move out. It only took me twenty-five years to get out of my dad's basement. Side note, it was my man cave through all five years of high school and five years of college, and then all of a sudden when I was twenty-five, he gave me an ultimatum: Mow the lawn or move out. So, I got a sweet studio apartment with my girlfriend Lauren. Now she's nagging me to wash my dishes, fold my underwear, pitch in for rent, and get a job. Geez, I would've stayed home if I knew she was going to lay down the law. Anyways, since I've been smart with my money by sponging off others for so long, I've squirreled away a nice chunk of cash to buy a condo. The housing lingo is super confusing, like mortgage, interest, amortization, and down payment. Where do I start?

Signed,

Jilted James

Dear JJ,

Wow, you are quite a catch. Lauren must be a patient woman! Buying your first home is exciting, terrifying, and gratifying. Let's assume you have a good stable job, just for kicks. Let's also imagine you have an excellent credit score. Finally, let's presume you have 10–20 percent of the purchase price as a down payment. Lots of assumptions, which are really speculation on my part! If your condo costs $400,000, then you'll need around $40–50,000 as a down payment. You will then have to get a mortgage (housing loan) from a financial institution to pay the rest. Essentially, they will loan you the money for fifteen or thirty years, and you'll pay them back with a mortgage payment each month in a similar amount to what you might be paying for a rent payment. It's a big commitment, and a lot of thought should go into where you want to live, how much you can spend, and how long you expect to be in the home. I've bought nine homes over my lifetime, and one thought that always guided me was "Would someone else want to buy this when we move?" If the answer is yes, then it might be a good idea.

Chapter 12

FINALLY, IT'S MY ROOF AND NOT DAD'S!

"As long as you're under my roof, you'll follow my rules. Blah blah blah and other things you won't have to hear from your dad."

— Johnny B

THE YEAR IS 2007. Apple introduced the first iPhone (side note, it would've been better to buy the stock back then, not the phone). NASA sent the Phoenix Mars Lander to ... Mars. It landed in 2008, which was amazing! And the unraveling of the economy was happening as the housing crisis/mortgage debacle was underway. We just didn't see it coming yet. Later in 2008, Lehman Brothers, a global financial services firm founded in 1847, with twenty-five thousand employees worldwide, filed for bankruptcy. The Lehman bankruptcy is thought by many to be the start of the financial crisis that began in 2008 and crippled the economy for several years. Many of you were in middle school or high school, and maybe as a family, you had to cut back on a few items. That house that your parents bought at the top of the market in 2007 was now losing value. *Hey JB, why all the doom and gloom?* Because it helps to remember history and learn from it.

In three years, from 2019 to 2021, the housing market soared around the country. I mean skyrocketed upward, like my jumping ability back in middle school. Okay, my vertical leap has never been that great, but I vividly remember dunking a tennis ball on a seven-foot basketball hoop back when I was twelve. My point is it felt like the housing market in the early 2020s could only go up. I guarantee it will not always go up, but if you like the town you're in, maybe it's time to buy a place.

MAKING IT YOURS

Now you are entering phase three of living under a roof.

Phase 1: You had to live under your dad's roof, but your rent was free.

Phase 2: You rented an apartment with friends. No "Dad rules," but now you pay rent.

Phase 3: Buying a home. No parents. Probably no friends in the home, at least not long term. All the fun/costs are yours!

Your first home will not be your last home, and most families move every seven years or less. Let me repeat that ... Your first home will not be your last home, and most families move every seven years or less. If you think about it in those terms, then buy the best place you can that you like and that the next family to buy it after you will also like.

Rent Versus Own

	Advantage	Disadvantage
Renting	Limited financial obligation	No equity growth or store of value
	Limited maintenance expenses	Lifestyle limitations (no pets, no garden, noise cur-few!)
	More liquidity	Decorating/renovating limitations
	More mobility	Less predictable housing expenses
Owning	Store of value and possible equity growth	Substantial financial obligation
	Lifestyle choices	Significant annual expenses
	Decorating/renovating choices	Less liquidity
	Pride of ownership	Less mobility
	Tax deduction for mortgage interest	
	More predictable housing expenses	

Entire books have been written about buying a home, and for me to cover the topic in a couple of pages will be like dipping our toes in the water. I want to cover a few topics, and the chart gives a good synopsis of what you should consider. If you think buying a car is exciting and emotional, wait until you start the home-buying process!

My goal soon after getting married in the 1990s was to get a home with a yard. Your goal may be a condo, a camper van, or a brownstone in the city. Whatever you think you want, remember that you may only be there for five years, so think of the next buyer, too. The first home we bought was a modest one-level ranch in Portland, Oregon, near the Nike World Campus. Seven moves later, it is still probably my favorite home because of its simplicity and the private yard. We paid $95,000 for it, and at the time, it was scary as hell because we were stretching for the down payment. I had no idea what a mortgage was or how to fix anything. My neighbor was an old codger named Ed, who would sit on his stool in the driveway, smoking packs of cigarettes and critiquing my lawn-mowing ability between our properties. He was kind of scary, but he would always lend me a hand or a tool when I needed it. What's even scarier is that his forty-year-old son Kevin lived in the basement, but that's another story.

Let's start with a mortgage. Funny word, I always thought, and what does it mean? A mortgage is your loan on the house. If you buy a condo for $250,000 and you put 10 percent down ($25,000), then your mortgage is $225,000. Is your mortgage your only monthly cost on the house? NO. Pity the fool (cheesy Mr. T reference) who doesn't get to know their PITI!

Principal: your mortgage loan amount or how much you owe

Interest: the money charged for the cost to borrow

Taxes: property and local taxes to pay for schools, roads, and government services

Insurance: costs to replace or repair your home in case of fire, flood, or major storms

And maintenance! Oh, the maintenance and repairs. I'm not trying to discourage you from buying a home, because that is a significant rite of passage into adulting. But buying a home does have costs and headaches, though ultimately, you will experience the satisfaction of fixing (or attempting to fix) some stuff yourself.

HOUSE MATH

Buying a home is a huge deal, so we're just going to focus on the math. You know you can search online, find the neighborhood, research the schools, and reluctantly talk to that annoying realtor (who seems to follow you down the aisles in the grocery store) to get some home ideas. But we are going to talk about the monthly dollar amount you'll have to cover. Lenders (mortgage companies, banks, your rich Aunt Pammie in South Florida) do their own calculations of how much debt you can afford. Whoever lends you money generally figures that no more than 33 percent of your gross income should go toward your monthly housing costs or PITI. If you have other loans, such as for your car or your education, then that total number (all those loans included) could be about 38 percent of your gross income.

It's stressful. It's a lot of math. It's worth it! However, don't fall into the FOMO crowd just to get a home. Just because Drew and Rebecca are buying a lovely three-bedroom townhome with a manicured lawn doesn't mean you have to. Maybe you'd rather travel. Maybe you want to live in Ireland. Maybe you want to buy a camper van, work remote, and travel the country posting videos of your excursions. There's no rush, but when you're ready, run the numbers. Other considerations:

- Will your spouse continue to work after you have that second child?
- Will you stay in the community, or could you move across the country?
- Do you want to take care of the home yourself, or would you rather call maintenance when the furnace gives out in February?
- Is your job with a solid company in a stable industry, and will they want to keep you?

Certainly, you won't know all these answers, but they are worth considering. Most of the time, you are giving your best guess on how the future may unfold. Even if you think you know what may happen, curveballs will always come your way. With all of that factored in ... owning your home brings pride and a certain satisfaction that you aren't just tossing your money away in rent.

On the flip side, you could just rent. It's kind of counterintuitive, but renting, you understand. You've already rented a crappy house in college with two of your best buddies and that odd third gal who drank your seltzers, dried her laundry all over the house, and never cleaned the kitchen. You know the rental experience with roomies and eventually living alone. Something breaks, then you call maintenance. Pay the rent and utilities each month, and hope they don't raise your rent each year. Piece of cake.

You must consider a lot of factors when making your first home purchase. Run the numbers and bring in Dad. He'll give you countless anecdotes of all the repairs he's made over the years and what they cost. Don't forget to bring in Mom's point of view, which is a heavy dose of reality on what is really important to look for in a home, including school districts, layout, and the surrounding community. Don't stretch too far on the payments, even though the bank will entice you to borrow more. And remember this first home isn't your last home, so get one that you mostly like and that you can fix up for the next family that you sell it to.

$\equiv$*GOBIT$*

GOBIT #23: Take all that budget stuff that I sneakily taught you a few chapters ago and figure out what type of home you can afford. If you don't know a mortgage lender, talk to a trusted friend or family member, and they can introduce you to someone. Research what you can afford before you start looking. The fun part is looking, and once you start, it is hard to turn it off. Walk away from a deal if it doesn't check almost all your boxes regarding price, location, and style.

GOBIT #24: Work with professionals on your first home. Realtors, lenders, CPAs, and attorneys, if needed, who were introduced to you by trusted friends. Don't go it alone to save a few bucks. On your third or fourth home down the road, you'll get the process and maybe won't need a realtor, but their commission is often worth the peace of mind.

PART IV:
SAFEGUARD YOURSELF
AND YOUR STUFF

DADS CAN SEE THE FUTURE. Did I forget to mention that in the earlier chapters? Yep, we can pretty much predict the future with moderate success in a handful of situations. For example, I know that as a husband, I will say something stupid at least twice a week that will get me in trouble with my wife. However, I also knew the first time I met my wife that she'd be my future wife! She didn't know it yet, and it took about five years of convincing. I knew as my kids started to drive that one, if not both, of our cars would have an unexplained dent from their driving within the first year. I knew every time I got in the car, the gas tank would be empty. And finally, I knew that my daughter's first boyfriend in seventh grade was not "the one," even though her mom thought he was "so darn cute." Yah, we can see a lot of things that will happen in the future.

Unfortunately, our ability to predict the future did not trans-late into buying a whole bunch of Apple stock when they first introduced the iPod back in 2001. If instead of buying an iPod, you bought $1,000 worth of Apple stock, then it would now be worth around $425,000.⁸ Oops! In reality, nobody really knows what's around the corner, so it's best to protect yourself before the unforeseen happens. Something will happen at some point, and if you don't have a plan or insurance, you'll have to foot the entire bill.

If you don't invest in your retirement when you're young, then you'll be working the rest of your life to keep up. If you don't keep an eye on your credit cards, then they could overtake your life. If you don't have insurance to protect your health, your home, and your stuff, then when something happens, it's all up to you to pay the bill.

Think of insurance as sharing the bill with someone at dinner. When the final tab comes after countless appetizers and a few drinks, it's nice when everyone chips in. Except for that tightwad Jeff, who always seems to misplace his credit card, gets T-rex arms when the bill comes, and conveniently forgets to Venmo everyone the next day. Let's not invite Jeff anymore! Anyway, insurance companies split the bill with you if you wreck your car, break an arm, or the dishwasher explodes while you're at your axe-throwing league on Tuesday night.

Get protection for yourself and your stuff and pay the monthly or annual bill. I know you'll wonder why you have it if you never seem to use insurance, but the one time you need it, you'll be glad you're covered.

I'm kind of a Big Deal. Softball teams, employers, chat rooms, and of course, dance competitions all want a piece of me. Every time I get a new job, another recruiter comes knocking to tell me about a new gig. Of course, I listen, and ultimately, I end up "taking my talent" to the highest bidder. While the increased pay is usually nice, I do have three or four old 401(k)s from these unlucky former employers. Should I just cash them in, or what do I do with them?

Signed,

Big Deal Dan

Dear Big D,

Wow, you're not lacking in job offers or confidence! DO NOT CASH IN YOUR OLD 401(k)s! If you do, Uncle Sam will want his tax cut and a 10 percent early distribution penalty. This could cut 40–50 percent off your total. Open your own IRA, and you can consolidate all your 401(k)s into one IRA. If you have any Roth money, you can consolidate that into a Roth IRA. You could also leave the money in your old 401(k)s if permitted. Or you could roll over the money to your new employer if rollovers are permitted. Be smart about your old 401(k)s, and you really could be a Big Deal.

Chapter 13

FREE MONEY:
Protect Your Retirement

"To Roth or not to Roth ...
so many questions."

— Johnny B

IF I REALLY WANTED TO GRAB YOUR ATTENTION, I'd stand at your front door with cash. Free money! Minimal obligation, and it will make your life dramatically better in forty years. What's the catch? You must sign up for your work retirement plan and contribute at least the minimum to get the company match. The idea is to protect your future self by contributing to your retirement account today.

Huh?

It's simple, actually, and "easy," but many individuals put off their retirement accounts or just ignore them because that phase of life is decades down the road. By adding money each paycheck to your retirement account, you are protecting your way of life in retirement. Protect how you choose to spend retirement versus how you may be forced to live in retirement if you run out of money.

Forty years from now, your car won't have a steering wheel and your vehicle will hover you to your favorite juice bar/brewery/cyclebar in a matter of seconds. Forty years from now, somebody will mountain bike up Mount Everest. Forty years from now, President Bieber will have dance parties in the White House. Forty years from now, you may be retired. Weird, right?!

Why is the retirement age sixty-five? Fun fact: The original Social Security Act of 1935 set the minimum age for receiving full retirement benefits at sixty-five.[9] Seemed like a reasonable number, except that back in the 1930s, '40s, and '50s, people retiring at sixty-five tended to die soon after. Nowadays, instead of inhaling fried eggs in bacon grease for breakfast, we sip on kale protein smoothies. In lieu of driving to the corner tavern for a couple of boilermakers, today we jog to an oxygen bar. Yes, we have that daily battle to be healthier, which translates into most humans, on average, living longer. So instead of kicking off at sixty-five, we are living into our eighties. If you retire in your sixties, you may be above ground for twenty years or more. What's my point? I may have mentioned this before, but you have to save for retirement because the government isn't going to take care of you, even though the politicians like to tell you otherwise.

So, when you think about retirement, don't focus on the fact that it's so far away that we might have flying cars and The Bieber in the White House. Think of it as the most awesome vacation ever! And you're saving to take that vacation. Now I've got your attention. The most awesome vacation ever starts when you retire! It's so awesome that sometimes you run out of things to do. Should you play pickleball, take a nap, volunteer at Little League Baseball, walk the mall, complain about politicians, or travel to Italy? When you retire, if you've saved over your lifetime, you can do all those things!

Whenever that target age is for retirement: sixty-five, fifty, thirty-five if you're a professional tennis player, twenty-five if you're an Olympic swimmer, twenty if you're a gymnast, or fifteen if you're a TikTok phenom. Let's shoot for sixty-five-ish and back into what you need to do now.

THE GIFT OF FREE MONEY

You have several options for saving for retirement. In a few paragraphs, I'm going to describe each one, so don't lose interest and start scrolling your social media just yet. And then we'll get into whether you should choose to Roth or not to Roth. Hold on, I know you're getting excited, but don't read ahead. I know how hyped up you are to learn about pre-tax and after-tax contributions. Sit down, close your Snapchat, and focus for another four and a half minutes.

The difference between a Roth retirement contribution and a regular contribution has to do with when you pay taxes. Uncle Sam, a.k.a. the government, a.k.a. Big Brother, will grab his taxes at some point. Either when you put the money in a retirement account with after-tax money, or in retirement when you are taxed for taking money out of a retirement account. I feel you glazing over and sinking into your bean bag, so just understand that you will pay taxes at some point. Let's dive in ...

TRADITIONAL 401(K) PLANS AND IRAS

If you work for an employer that offers a 401(k) (or 403(b) at a public institution), then sign up and contribute. Do it! Now! Don't respond to that next text until you sign up. In 2022, you can contribute up to $19,500 pre-tax in your 401(k). As I've mentioned, your employer may offer to match some of your contributions, like 3 percent of your salary, for example. Let's say you make $50,000, for easy math. You put in $10,000, and now your taxable income is only $40,000 for the year. And your employer contributes another $1,500 (3 percent of $50,000) for you because they like you and want to keep you. Your total pre-tax contribution is $11,500 and should increase as your wages increase. When you retire, you will be taxed at the future income tax rates when you pull money out for food, travel, or the latest pickleball sportswear.

If you're in your fourth job and third career as you're pushing thirty, you may have several old 401(k)s and random IRAs (individual retirement accounts). Most likely, you can combine them into one IRA for simplicity. If you don't have a 401(k) with your employer, then you can put $6,000 per year pre-tax into an IRA (in 2022—the amount may change). There are rules and limitations based on income limits, so check the current details before contributing. With an IRA, like your 401(k), you will be taxed at retirement when you pull money out. If you don't have a 401(k), then open an IRA. Today!

ROTH 401(K)

A Roth 401(k) follows the same example, but now your contribution is using after-tax money. You don't get the immediate tax deduction, but when you take money out in retirement, you owe no taxes. Zero, notta, zippo! If your company has this Roth option, then consider weighting more toward Roth while your income is lower. The idea is that your income taxes may be lower now than in retirement. You could choose to split 75 percent of your contribution into your Roth 401(k) and 25 percent into your traditional 401(k), as an example. Again, every worker has a different financial situation, so talk to your HR rep, a trusted financial planner, or even good ole Dad.

ROTH IRA

Similar to a Roth 401(k), your contributions are after-tax. So, that means ... bingo! You are contributing with money you've already paid taxes on. Your money will grow tax-free, and at retirement, you can take money out without paying Uncle Sam again. You're catching on! In 2022, you can put in $6,000 per year. There are limitations based on your income and other retirement benefits, so read the fine print on the IRS website (haha, I know you won't, but this is where the info will be) or get some guidance from a trusted professional.

SEP IRA

And last but not least is another option for an IRA if you are a gig worker. Food delivery, Lyft driver, writer, or some other independent contractor who pays all your own taxes.

If you have a side hustle, a.k.a. being self-employed, you can establish a SEP IRA. A Simplified Employee Pension IRA has all the same qualities of a traditional IRA, but you can possibly contribute more than $6,000 per year. The rules allow you to contribute up to 25 percent of your income with a cap of $61,000 in 2022.[10] These numbers change yearly, so the next time you are scanning the IRS website, in between binge-watching *Gray's Anatomy*, just for kicks, check out the latest percentages and caps on contributions. Obviously a $61,000 pre-tax contribution is assuming your income is about $240,000, which may be high for a side hustle but realistic if you have your own business with no employees. Anyway ... lots of rules with a SEP, but I wanted to mention it in case it is a better option for you.

IS YOUR HEAD SPINNING YET?

This can be confusing, but it is very, very important. Do not put this off like laundry, dental cleanings, and oil changes. If you have a retirement plan at work, then maximize that option first. If you have a side hustle or just want to understand your options, then research the above options at irs.gov/retirement-plans. This site will have the most current rules and limits. If going to a government website makes you want to scream in your pillow, enlist your MoneyBuddy, your dad, or a trusted advisor to help you navigate your options.

Back to the *free money*! The very least you should do if you have a retirement plan at work is contribute at least the minimum to get the free match from your employer. I absolutely want you to contribute more than the minimum, but I understand if funds are tight and all you can do is the minimum to get the company match. Way too many employees focus on whether their new job has a barista, free lunches, remote workdays, and a nap room. All of those perks are nice, but a free match for your retirement plan is huge. If I haven't pounded it into your head yet, make sure you are taking full advantage of it. Time to get started. Sign up and forget about it for a year and then review your money each January and June, or about when you get your next oil change for your car.

GOBIT$

GOBIT #25: Go to your HR intranet site at work and learn about your 401(k). What are your options with traditional and Roth contributions? What is the company match? What are your investment options? How often can you make changes? When does this benefit start—immediately, after thirty days, or after twelve months? What is the vesting schedule, which means when does the company match become truly yours? Most of the time, the company match will vest one-third each year, so if you change companies, you may not get all the match. Your contributions are always 100 percent yours to do with as you wish. Get clarity from the HR team.

GOBIT #26: Actively save for your retirement by making it a passive process. Stick with me for a moment ... Figure out an amount you'll need for retirement. One, two, five million?! And then figure out how much you would need to save each month to get there. Most of your company 401(k) plans have a retirement calculator that can help with the math. Start with whatever you can—$50 to $500 per paycheck—and defer/transfer/move it into a savings account. Start now! Yes, this is like the seventeenth time I've said this, but it's critical. Get started and keep up the momentum.

How can I score better? No, I'm not talking about my golf scorecard or anything crude, for that matter. I finally have a real job with decent income, but my credit score still sucks. I haven't done anything wrong, I swear! Maybe I was a month or two behind on a few credit card payments, but that was back in college. I am a model citizen now with a car, a home, and a significant other that likes me most of the time. How can I get the "credit man" off my back and boost my score?

Signed,

The Honorable Hudson

Dear The Honorable Hudson,

You're on the right path when you're thinking about boosting and protecting your score. Contact the credit bureaus and clean up any errors in your report. I never lived in Michigan, but a credit report said I did. I had it removed. Also, build your credit history slowly with a zero-fee credit card. Use it wisely, my young Jedi, and pay it off each month. Always. Forever. A good track record will slowly increase your credit score and help you get future credit at a lower interest rate.

Chapter 14

OTHER PEOPLE'S MONEY:
Protect Your Credit

"Credit cards unfortunately allow us to buy
dumb things that we don't need a month
before we have the money to pay for them."

— Johnny B

BACK WHEN I WAS YOUR AGE (it's been a few chapters since I blurted this statement, so relax) ... *I know, I know, you used to walk uphill both ways in the frozen slush through blinding blizzards with no shoes or coat. We've heard how miserably difficult life was in the seventies and eighties before Netflix and Chipotle.* That actually is not where I was going, but it never hurts to remind Millennials that we had to drive to Blockbuster for videos, and pizza was the only food that was delivered.

Again, back to when I was nearing my Super Senior year in college, with very few job prospects, I was suddenly inundated with credit card offers. *Big whoop*, you say, *every college student gets those*, but I didn't know that. I thought the financial elite saw something special in me and wanted to grant me the opportunity to buy necessities on credit. Since I was a poor college kid with a couple of part-time jobs, this newfound power was encouraging.

I told myself I was only going to use my shiny new credit card when I really needed it. I mean, I was cheap and studied finance in business school, so of course I knew how to manage my money. Right? Probably wouldn't ever need to use it. And then in the late eighties, an awesome, new *must-have* bicycle was sweeping the college campuses: the mountain bike.

Of course, everyone living in Lawrence, Kansas, the home of the University of Kansas, is keenly aware that the campus is on a mountain. Mount Oread (not lying, Google it, I swear. Though some would consider it a short hill). I convinced myself I should research this new two-wheeler since I kind of "needed" one for transportation to get to my jobs and campus. Ironically, the bike shop had one left in my XL size. It was a sweet Schwinn red-white-blue King of the Mountain. Conveniently, it was priced half off $1,000. $500! Weirdly, my credit limit was $500, so it was essentially a perfect match. What a deal! I couldn't pass it up. I pulled the trigger and bought my new two-wheeler in college with my nifty new little piece of plastic. I had no idea how to pay for it since my total income was about $500 a month and I had to pay for rent, food, and an occasional adult beverage, which meant I had zero dollars left over at the end of the month.

Twenty-eight days later, I got my first monthly credit card bill. The balance said $500, but they only asked me to pay $23. Well heck, I can swing $23 somehow. Easy-peasy. I had no idea I was making the minimum payment and I was accruing interest charges in excess of 25 percent each month. At that rate, I would have it paid off when my future great-grandkids were ready to ride bikes.

In reality, I borrowed $500 to buy the bike. I made payments for several years and eventually paid more than $1,100 in total after interest and late fees. Not a good deal. If you can't pay off your credit card balance each month, then *don't use it*. Great memories of that bike. I still have most of it thirty years later, less a few tires and a chain, but I can't toss it because it taught me a great financial lesson.

CREDIT AIN'T FREE (BUT IT CAN BE HELPFUL)

The average APR (annual percentage rate) for brand-new credit cards held steady again as of February 2023, remaining at 16.13 percent for the twelfth week in a row, according to the CreditCards.com Weekly Credit Card Rate Report.[11]

Don't kid yourself with credit cards. It's not your money. It's the bank's money. Cash is your money. Credit cards are loans. Loans from banks that are very happy to give you a new shiny piece of plastic each year so you'll pull it out for every purchase. But credit cards can get you in a lot of trouble if you don't manage them each month.

Enough of the scare tactics. I'm not saying to avoid all credit cards. In fact, they can help you immensely with your personal finances.

- Credit cards can help you establish a credit score. Good credit scores will help you finance larger purchases like refrigerators, cars, and homes down the road.
- Credit cards can keep your purchases organized in categories.
- Credit cards may have travel rewards or cash back that can add up.

YOU ONLY NEED ONE

Where do you start? If you and your spouse are gainfully employed, then you probably only need one card, maybe two. You don't need a gas card, grocery card, airline card, Lululemon card, and a Star Trek credit card for you Trekkies. Pick one with low or no fees and cut up and cancel the rest that gave you a free burrito when you signed up. More is not better, and it can sometimes hurt your credit rating if you have too many credit cards (a.k.a. lines of credit open). Keep it simple.

The average American carried two credit cards and had a total outstanding balance of $6,270 in 2021.[12] As Momma always told you, don't be average! Have your main credit card and maybe, just maybe, a backup with no annual fee in case you need it for an emergency. And absolutely, always, without exception, pay off your monthly balance in full every month!

WHAT ABOUT DEBIT?

And finally, I thought I'd touch on credit cards versus debit cards. By now you've grown up with a debit card. You get how it works. You swipe your debit card, and the money leaves your bank account right away. If that helps you manage your finances, then stick to the debit card. The credit card adds the benefit of fighting identity theft on purchases or just a defective product that you want to return. Credit card companies allow you to contest charges on your monthly statement, while your debit card money has already left your account at the time of purchase. Are you following me? Once the money leaves your bank account, it's awfully hard to get it back if you want to dispute a charge.

PAY OFF – PAY OFF – PAY OFF your credit card every month, and you won't run into trouble. Your credit score will improve and go up. You'll have more of a credit history. Everything is sunshine and unicorns. Miss a few payments, and the 25 percent interest rate will rack up debt fast, your credit history will get cloudy, and your unicorn will run away.

Don't forget that credit is good and necessary, but it is the bank's money. Treat it like other people's money and pay it back on schedule, and you'll be fine. Don't be an average American and rack up high-interest credit card debt. Pay off your bills on time, every time.

GOBIT$

GOBIT #27: You probably have at least one credit card. Do you really need a Best Buy, Kohl's, Athleta, and Dunkin' credit card? Pick a versatile bank credit card with no annual fee, like Visa, MasterCard, or Discover, and shred and cancel the others. Pay it off, in full(!), every month. *Always*. Set a goal of six consecutive months, then twelve, and so on. This will drive up your credit score.

GOBIT #28: Get your free credit report every January. You are entitled to a free report from each credit reporting agency each year. Go to annualcreditreport.com and make your first request. If some hacker tries to steal your identity, these reports might be the first place you see it. This is a great way to keep an eye on your finances and make sure you don't have any unknown accounts attached to you.

Those car insurance commercials make me chuckle. Can I really save 15 percent or more? Maybe I can, but it seems like a lot of effort to research all my options. First, I have to find my phone. Then I have to ask Siri to search car insurance and then sift through all the companies. You're probably going to want me to create a stupid spreadsheet comparing all my options. Is it really worth the effort?

Signed,

Lazy Lisa

Dear Lazy Lisa,

I know shopping for car insurance ranks up there with changing your windshield wipers, but ... an annual price check is a great way to save money. Go beyond the commercials and find the company that is best for you and your budget. Ask that frugal uncle because his least favorite expense is car insurance, and he'll be glad to gloat about how he researched long and hard to find the ideal insurance company.

Chapter 15

WRAP THAT RASCAL WITH INSURANCE:
Protect Your Stuff

"Have someone else share in your
mishaps. Buy insurance."

— Johnny B

LIFE IS RISKY. You could ski into a tree, by accident. Your car could slide into another car, by accident. Your laptop and Xbox could get waterlogged because the dipstick in the apartment above you forgot to turn off the bathtub and the bathwater seeped through your ceiling and onto your electronics, by accident. You can try to avoid accidents, but you can't eliminate them. You can, however, pay someone to share in the cost when you have an accident. That, my friend, is insurance.

WE BUY INSURANCE, AND SOMETIMES IT PAYS US BACK

You can purchase insurance to protect your important gear, your home, your health, your income, your car, and your life. If you bundle it all together like the little lizard demands of you in countless commercials, it may save you money. Shopping for insurance has gotten incredibly easier and more confusing. Say what?! How much do you need? And of course, where do you get it from? As a human for fifty-plus years wandering this planet, I have reluctantly bought a lot of insurance and gladly received the benefits of a lot of insurance. Here's a short list of why I appreciate having insurance:

* Our house flooded because the washing machine hose broke off—$5 part caused $30,000+ worth of damage. Covered.
* Family car totaled. My son was okay. Thank you, airbags!—$9,000 worth of damage. Covered.
* Hail damage on our cars and house roof multiple times—$50,000+ in damage. Covered.
* Family medical bills, prescriptions, and ER countless times. Thousands and thousands of dollars. Who knows how much I've spent on myself and the family over the years. Covered.

Any dad could go on and on whining about paying for insurance over several decades and then in the same sentence, express gratitude that it was there when he needed it. It is the least fun thing to purchase because you can't see it, smell it, drive it, or take selfies with it. But you need it, and you must get it. I'm going to break insurance down into a few categories and explain to you why you need it. If you don't buy it, then you are on the hook for 100 percent of whatever happens. Just get it so you have a partner to share in the costs of an accident. That's right—because it just makes sense!

31 FLAVORS

Maybe not thirty-one different kinds of insurance for personal needs, but there are quite a few, so let's highlight the important ones you need to have.

Bubble Wrap That Car with Insurance

It's a no-brainer, and the law! Insurance will pay to fix major damage to your car or replace it if necessary.

Car insurance can be very confusing, but with online shopping, you can learn which policy is best for you without leaving your hammock. I could write an entire book about car insurance, but I'm sure you would toss it out a moving vehicle and hope it gets trampled, so I'll just hit the highlights.

Comprehensive: This means that you are covered if you have a car accident and it is your fault. You, your car, and whomever you crash into will be covered and reimbursed for damages minus the deductible. This is good to have if you have a newer, low-mileage car.

Deductible: If your deductible is $500, you have to pay the first $500 of the repair bill. If your deductible is $1,000, then you pay the first $1,000. The higher the deductible, the lower your annual insurance premium because you are covering more of the liability. It may make sense to increase your deductible on high-mileage or older cars because they are less costly to repair.

Liability only: If your car is older and has 100,000+ miles on it, then maybe you only need to cover repairs to the other car that you "bumped" on the expressway. With liability only, if you crunch another car as you're running a yellowish/red light, and it's your fault, liability-only coverage will pay for their damage once you meet your deductible. If there's damage to your car, you are not covered, and you have to pony up for the repair bill. This coverage tends to be significantly cheaper than full coverage and might be worth considering if you have an older, high-mileage car.

Wrap Yourself with Health Insurance

It seems like another no-brainer. If you're single, get it. If you and your spouse both have good jobs with health insurance, then compare the two side by side. The cheapest might not be the best option if it doesn't offer the same benefits. If you're young and healthy, consider a high deductible plan with a Health Savings Account. This plan will give you catastrophic coverage if you have a major medical emergency, and you can build up savings in a tax-free account for medical expenses. If you have a family with kids, then a standard PPO or HMO plan may fit you best. If you are a gig worker, you'll have to get your plan through your state. I highly suggest you get something in place so you can cover a catastrophic emergency.

Wrap Your Home and Important Stuff with Homeowners and Renters' Insurance

Renters' insurance replaces your electronics, clothes, stand-up paddleboard, and other valuables. Why get it? Let's say your apartment building burns to the ground. The owner will have insurance to rebuild, but it doesn't cover your stuff. Same goes if your items get stolen. This insurance is typically only a few hundred dollars a year, so it's cheap. Get it!

If you own your home, you have to get homeowners insurance because the mortgage company requires it. You want to make sure you have enough coverage to replace your home or your personal items in case of fire, flood, hail, or theft. I could write another book that would cause you to slip into a coma, but the idea is to review your policy every year to make sure you have proper coverage.

Wrap Your Future Income with Disability Insurance

"DI," as we like to call it in the financial biz, is something you buy to replace your income if you can't work. I mentioned this earlier in the book, but it is worth repeating. This is too often overlooked during open enrollment, and it should be at the top of your list. If you cannot work for an extended period because of an injury or illness, then DI will replace most of your income. Typically, with larger employers, it is included in your health coverage, but look into the details to make sure you have it.

Wrap Your Loved One's Future with Life Insurance

And last but not least is insurance to replace your future income if you expire prematurely. Life insurance is not for you to enjoy! It is for your loved ones to replace your income and pay your bills if you're six feet under, a.k.a. dead! Again, most larger companies will provide you with 1X or 2X of your annual salary as a benefit. That is probably okay until you get married and start having little humans that look like you running around the house. How much you get depends on your income, age, debt obligations, and family. Most likely, at a young age (under forty), all you need is term insurance for some time period. Twenty-year term insurance means you pay the same annual premium for twenty years, and then it expires. This is the cheapest, and it will protect you if something unfortunate happens.

AND THAT'S A WRAP!

I am so proud of you for learning about insurance these last fifteen minutes. My goodness, look at how you've matured since page one of this little booklet. Now you can go out and impress your friends at your next improv class with your newfound knowledge. And if you're awkwardly cornered at the next holiday party by Karly in accounting discussing the latest in Excel pivot tables, you can break out the intricacies of disability insurance, and maybe she'll wander off.

≡GOBIT$

GOBIT #29: Be an active insurance consumer. Sounds like fun, doesn't it? This means reviewing your policies at least once every two years. Dads have very few faults, but I know many dads who haven't looked at their policies in decades, which could be costing them hundreds a month. Your dad will complain about gas going up a nickel a gallon, but even he forgets to regularly check his insurance policies because he signed up with his college buddy thirty years ago. Search and find your current insurance documents—car, home, and rental—and evaluate your policies. Yes, it sounds awful, but you could save hundreds or thousands, as the annoying commercials preach. If you don't want to research on your own, then find an insurance agent via friends or family, and they will compare policies for you. And employ your dad to help because this is a great way to save money, and you might even teach the old man a thing or two.

GOBIT #30: Health insurance is a little harder to compare, but don't forget about it. Once a year is open enrollment with your employer or the government, depending on where you get your coverage. Take a few hours to understand your options, and contact your HR person if you have questions. Don't wait until 11:59 p.m. the day before you must decide. If you're young and healthy, you can probably lean toward a high deductible plan with an HSA account to save money, but do your homework at least once a year. If you are a gig worker, then look to your state government and their health exchange for discounts and policies.

I love my future hubby, Zach. It is mind-boggling how talented he is at tossing the frisbee, fantasy football, and beer pong. And did I mention he makes amazing avocado toast every third Saturday when he gets up before noon? Despite these amazing talents, he is a financial disaster, and without me, I think he'd be in a van down by the river. Which, by the way, he'd be okay with. Should I pull a credit report on my fiancé?

Signed,

The Responsible One

Dear Responsible One,

Um ... that's a definite yes! Zach sounds like he has some fantastic qualities for a college freshman, but his financial acumen is lacking. Probably his dad's fault. Print off his credit report. Review it with him, and maybe give him a hug. If he's in the 300s, it's not a deal breaker, but he's going to need some hand-holding and financial discipline. While you're at it, pull your own credit report at the start of each year to make sure you don't have any unknown accounts popping up.

Chapter 16

LOVE AND MONEY:
Protect Yourself

"If you had to choose between true
love or traveling the world, which
country would you visit first?"

— Johnny B

I'M NOT ADVOCATING FOR A LIFE OF bachelorhood or
spinsterhood. I seriously outkicked the coverage, leaned over my
skis, and just plain overachieved when it came to my amazing
wife, Carey. I'm a big fan of marriage. And it is a lot of hard work,
especially when it comes to financial matters. I'm not going to
advise you on all the other challenges men face with marriage,
like how to make a bed, put the toilet seat down, and find the
hamper for dirty socks. The acts of moving your dishes from the
counter to the dishwasher and putting the seat down are tough
adaptations that you may never master. More importantly, your

financial world will not magically take care of itself, as your money viewpoints will collide at some point.

You have to earn money, save money, spend money wisely, and make concessions and compromises daily. When you're single, you can blow your paycheck on a vintage ukulele or spur-of-the-moment trip to the Oregon Coast. You'll be all by yourself trying to figure out where to get your car brakes fixed and how much to spend on eating out. But once you have a partner, you may need to consult her if you purchase a new set of TaylorMade golf clubs or run it by him if you buy a Louis Vuitton purse. Option #2 is to try and sneak in that purchase and deal with the aftermath. Not advised. Speaking from experience!

Here are the top three ways to communicate with your partner about dinero, moolah, money:

- Send smoke signals to him that you bought new leather boots.
- Leave a sticky note on her steering wheel that you booked a guy's-only golf trip to Ireland.
- Get a joint checking account and joint credit card and have a healthy money talk at a reasonable fast-casual restaurant when your statements arrive each month.

Yes, Door #3 is the best option. Actually, I can't imagine going back into the dating world. What do the kids say today as they approach someone who looks date-worthy? "Hi, you're cute. What's your FICO score?" Not a pickup line you would've heard back in my day, but it might be your first line of questioning in today's world. You might want to give these other pickup lines a shot if you want to stay *single* ...

* Accounting is a numbers game, so why not give me yours?
* You and I are like nachos with jalapeños. I'm super cheesy, you're super hot, and we belong together.
* Are you a loan? Cause you've got my interest!

SHARING IS CARING

I'm sure the first date requests are all via text, Snapchat, or whatever social app is around the corner. Unfortunately, I fear men won't have the chance to get shut down, ridiculed, or just plain ignored in person for their feeble attempts to meet young ladies in the future because it will all transpire over their smartphones. However, your dating life may be evolving, and it's good to have an idea of who this other person is financially before you start sharing desserts and swapping bubble gum. It's a good idea to know before you walk down the aisle with Drew if he owns that condo, what his level of student debt really is, and if he goes to work every day or is just golfing with his buddies. And for Drew, it's a good idea to know if Rebecca shops the discount racks, has a respectable credit score, and wants to invest for the future long before you have Drew Junior crawling around the family room.

Love and money? Sounds like Valentine's Day, right? People spend over $886 million on their valentines.[13] Oh no, not on their partners but on their pets. One in five people bought Valentine's Day gifts for their pets, and almost half admit they cuddle with their dog more than they cuddle with their partner. So, you're telling me you prefer an animal that has bad breath, pees on the rug, and drinks from the toilet? I can't argue with that! But eventually, you may find someone who has the potential to stick around for a long time.

I'm not going to give you my shallow opinion on what you should look for in another human outside of the financial aspects. Short, tall, fat, skinny, funny, boring, type A, type B, or whatever piques your interest; give it a go. But too often, we forgo their financial acumen because "he's so funny" or "she's smokin' hot." If he's smelly and boring and constantly blurts out *Star Wars* trivia but seems really sharp with money, don't ghost him just yet. Let me go all Dad on you and look beyond the easy attributes and dig in to see if he pays his bills and has aspirations beyond being a part-time musician/barista/Lyft driver/video game tester.

If and when you finally get hitched, you will most likely eventually peek into your partner's finances and combine accounts. Let's say that Drew and Rebecca meet at a Saturday beach volleyball league, ride bikes every weekend, rescue an ugly mutt, share an SUV, and then decide to buy a condo together. Way before you get that ugly mutt, you should know if Drew is a financial disaster waiting to happen.

According to a recent bankrate.com survey, nearly half of all couples (43 percent) have at least one bank account that they share with their partner, while 23 percent have only separate accounts.[14] Of the generations surveyed, Millennial couples are the most likely to have separate accounts (69 percent). Debt can get you dumped! Respondents also said credit card debt would make them less likely to date a person.

It's a good thing my wife of thirty years didn't know I bought a mountain bike in college on my new fancy plastic credit card that I had no ability to pay back. One reason why credit card debt is so unappealing is that it may be a red flag of financial irresponsibility. Sure, I "needed" that mountain bike in college for transportation ... and five years later, I finally paid it off for twice the original price tag when you add up all the interest and late fees.

At some point, you will trip over that perfect match for you. Somehow, I found the perfect partner, so anything is possible. I'm not saying to demand that he reveal his credit score and online sports betting account before your first hike/date/brunch; however, if he forgets to pay rent but somehow owns $5,000 worth of classic vinyl records, then run! Not all financially challenged humans are undatable, but buyer beware and keep your options open.

Here's the really bad news. You will fight about money. Everyone in a marriage or serious relationship does. If you're lucky, it only happens once a year, maybe less. If it's happening every Tuesday, then you may want to find some outside guidance. Don't let money derail a great partnership, but also don't let it fester and explode.

GOBIT$

GOBIT #31: Conduct an in-depth, highly invasive background, credit, and website history check, plus research the person's Netflix favorites before even considering a first date. Okay, that's more of a dad's dream rule. But don't shy away from discussions about credit scores, student loan debt, and past bankruptcies when things get serious—and by "serious," I mean you'd consider using the other's toothbrush. In a pinch.

GOBIT #32: Already engaged or thinking it's on the horizon? Here are some things you need to agree on, today: kids, money, and Bigfoot. The first two are critical. The third will tell you if you'll have any fun in your marriage. Why kids and money? Because your views and habits will probably not change. I'll leave the number of kids, how many or none, to someone else. But money? Agree on joint or separate accounts—for checking, savings, and real savings (retirement). If one of you should be receiving an award from the ACA (American Cheapskate Association) and the other has seven maxed-out credit cards, six televisions, a snowmobile, a boat, a motorcycle, and a tanning bed, you might need to cast your line elsewhere.

PART V:
BUILD YOUR WEALTH

YOU'VE MADE IT. You're starting to hum along with a good job that pays well above your high school gig at the doggie daycare. Your living situation has improved from three roommates that you have outgrown because of their excessive video gaming and a scary bathroom situation that has some unidentifiable fungus creeping up the tile, down to single life with an occasional roommate who has long-term potential. Your finances are mildly under control with a respectable income, a budget for travel to all the weddings you're in, and semi-controllable expenses. Time to get on your scooter and coast through the next phase of your life! Right? Wrong!

Now the fun begins! Now is when you start to build your wealth. Flip back through the chapters that you read two hours or two months ago when your Grandma Rosie gave you this personal finance manual as a birthday gift. The number one class you did not take in college was personal finance, because it probably wasn't offered. I know it isn't offered because I teach personal finance at a local university in Colorado. The upper-class finance students reluctantly take it, but the rest of the student body has no idea it exists. Your money is your responsibility, even if you hate numbers and you're not very good with that sort of thing. I'm not asking you to be a legendary investor like Warren Buffett, but I'm also not going to let you bury your head in the sand and wake up at forty-five with no savings and touring the country in a VW Bus. Okay, I know for some of you, touring in a VW sounds perfect in your twenties, but if you're in your forties, then something in your financial world has gone sideways.

Let's pretend we are reviewing for a final. I know … I know you've put book textbooks behind you, and you've moved from PBRs to IPAs because you're more sophisticated. I've given you the study guide, and now it's up to you to continue to learn. I understand most of you will refuse to read the *Wall Street Journal* or even check your 401(k) account each quarter, but I'm just asking for a little financial awareness and consistency. Think of financial fitness like attempting to keep your college figure. It doesn't happen on its own, and you'll need to exert effort toward healthy living and a focused financial future.

In this final section, we'll explore investing and the next phase of your financial life. Think big, stay disciplined, and keep your eyes on the prize.

I'm so proud to have a target date for my next European Backpack Vacation and a target date for our annual hiking excursion in the Texas hill country. My calendar is filling up, but now I see these target-date funds in my 401(k)! Why should I care about these target dates?

Signed,

Proud Mary

Dear Proud Mary,

So many target dates, and so little time. A target-date fund in your 401(k) is designed to be a basket of mutual funds that coincides with your expected retirement at sixty-five. If you're twenty-five, your target-date allocation is much more aggressive because you have forty years to withstand market swoons. If you're fifty-five, your portfolio is more conservative. However, one size does not fit all. The manager of a target-date fund will automatically make changes every two to three years to make more conservative choices as you get older, and it may not offer the potential growth that an investor wants. Research your options and consult an advisor if you need help constructing your retirement account.

Chapter 17

INVESTING 1.0:
Be Boring

"Think of investing like your dad's Saturday
morning wardrobe. Embarrassingly boring."

— Johnny B

SCIENTISTS HAVE FIGURED OUT what makes you boring.[15]
I'm not kidding. Common characteristics of boring people are
that they are dull, not interesting, and inactive, and they have
zero sense of humor. Topping the list is that they are bad conver-
sationalists. There was a lot more to the study, but I was utterly
bored trying to read it. The funny thing is that this was not the
only study. There have been a bunch of studies about boring
people! OMG, can't we figure out how to put metal in the micro-
wave before we dive into why Jeffrey in the shipping department
is a terrible conversationalist? The point of my rant about boring
people is that I want you to Be Boring. Don't be Dull Danny during
your Thursday night co-ed soccer league or Longwinded Liam at

your Sunday brunch, but as far as your investment portfolio for retirement is concerned, I want you to dial down the enthusiasm a notch or two.

For Investing 1.0, I am only going to talk about investing for your retirement, or we could be here longer than trying to coach your dad on how not to run off buildings in *Call of Duty*. Investing 2.0 (in the next chapter) will pull the covers back and get more specific on what types of investment strategies you might consider. Out of all the Dadvice (Dad + Advice ... pretty clever, don't you think?) that I've been throwing at you over these last sixteen chapters, now I want you to really replicate your dad. No, no, I'm not suggesting that you go outside in cargo shorts, black socks, and your New Balance cross-trainers. I'm thinking less about the appearance of your average dad and more about his thought process. While you would rather go to an outdoor brewpub to play cornhole, your dad would rather chill on the back patio and enjoy his lite beer in a frosty mug. I'm guessing while you think trekking through Chile sounds unbelievably exciting, your dad is content walking the mall and devouring a Cinnabon. And you may think that day trading cryptocurrencies is investing, but your dad is happy as a clam to have a well-balanced, diversified portfolio that can withstand inevitable market downturns and be positioned to grow over time. Sometimes it's totally cool to be boring like your dad.

How does your pop do it? How does his portfolio grow over time and he not get too irritated with the dips in the markets? I'm going to let you in on a little secret about investing. Making money in the markets is relatively simple if you have a long horizon like ten-plus years. You have two options. Buy the perfect tech company stock when it has its Initial Public Offering, a.k.a.

IPOs (goes public), and watch it blow up like crazy. Then sell it at its absolute peak price (not likely). Or build a high-quality, diversified portfolio of low-cost ETFs and mutual funds, add to it each month, rebalance each year, and then use that nest egg to live off in retirement (more likely). Which path are you going to choose? Obviously, Option #1 sounds much more exciting, but so does winning the lottery. We all know that rarely happens, even though the talking heads on investment TV and chat rooms keep enticing you to follow their "proven" investment method. It's all BS!

LET'S GET DIVERSIFIED

Cue up *Physical* by Olivia Newton-John on your music app of the month. You may have to Google "Newton-John." She jump-started the headband and leg warmers fashion trend in the eighties, and more importantly, she was Sandy in *Grease*. Now you can hum "Let's get diversified" to yourself. Big word, I know, but *diversification* is a critical key to long-term success in investing.

Meet Sydney. Sydney is thirty and married, has two young kids, loves horses, and has a great job as an environmental engineer. She's married to Daniel, who is a mortgage banker, weekend golfer, and semi-pro bodybuilder. Quite the duo, right? Let's assume Sydney and Daniel want to have a cookout at their home out in the country. Daniel is dead set on serving a roasted pig for the lone entrée. Nothing else. That is it. No beans, salad, chips, or even cookies. Friends can BYOB and a BYO side if they want. Wow, isn't he quite the generous host! Sydney is a little more thoughtful and wants to put out a full spread to entice friends to actually show up and enjoy themselves.

Scenario #1

Daniel smokes the piggy all night and is ready to pull ole Porkchop off the smoker as gloomy guests arrive with their own drinks and homemade side dishes.

Scenario #2

Sydney is on the ball with a full buffet table of fried chicken, BBQ brisket, baked beans, chips, fruit salad, and cookies. She's stocked the trough with cold drinks for the adults and the little ones. And of course, she sets up horse rides and has little gift bags for the kiddos.

Nice story, JB. What's your point? My point is that when investing your hard-earned money for retirement, it's a good idea to review all your options before you choose your path. Let's assume Daniel's little piggy doesn't turn out so well. In fact, it's a disaster. Porkchop fell off the rack in the middle of the night, and now there are just charred bacon bits in the fire and no food for the arriving guests. Daniel bet all his success on Porkchop, and it didn't work out. Now he's scrambling. The kids and adults are hangry, his wife Sydney is pissed, and he's sulking behind the barn.

In Scenario #2, Sydney has everything ready plenty of time before the guests arrive. However, as she checks on the brisket, she realizes the temperature was too high, and it's now beef jerky! No fear because she has grilled chicken, side dishes, and cold beverages to save the day. Sydney had a well-diversified cookout (see what I did there), and even though the brisket went sideways, she was able to salvage a great afternoon, and the guests never knew.

I think you see where I'm going with this story. Don't put all your eggs in one basket. *Don't smoke just one pig!* Investing for retirement is no different. We want to keep the portfolio diversified, knowing that when one asset class is up, another one might be down. I know you want to curl up in a ball, bite your nails, or finish knitting that quilt for Nana's birthday instead of talking about investing, so I'm just going to focus on asset allocation.

GET YOUR ASS...ETS ALLOCATED

Hey Siri, how do you stay in shape?

(She answers in a British accent): Eat healthy, rest, and exercise.

The formula is really simple, but it is a challenge for most of us. Investing is no different. Let's assume your dad is thirty years older than you. His time horizon and appetite for risk in his retirement portfolio are very different from yours. How you invest for retirement in forty years can be vastly different from how you invest for a home down payment in four years. Your time horizon is one of the key factors, if not the most important factor, when investing. History tells us that while we have annual ups and downs in the stock market, in the long run (like ten-plus years invested), the US stock markets and most international stock markets have an upward trend. For long-term investors, this means don't be afraid of the stock market. Don't overthink investing in the stock market. Embrace it!

Let's go back to Sydney. Investing for retirement means Syd probably won't touch the money for forty years. I'm not kidding. Forty years. While Syd's pop is closer to retirement and his portfolio is more conservative and boring, Syd has decades to ride out the ups and downs of the markets, and she should not shy away from it. Yes, she's going to look at her 401(k) every quarter, but she doesn't need to make many changes other than to rebalance once a year. For example ... let's say (and I'm not recommending a portfolio for you because I don't know you or your personality or your appetite for risk or your time horizon or your favorite color or your favorite ice cream—is that enough of a disclaimer?), that you and Sydney have the same retirement investment allocation, and it looks like the following:

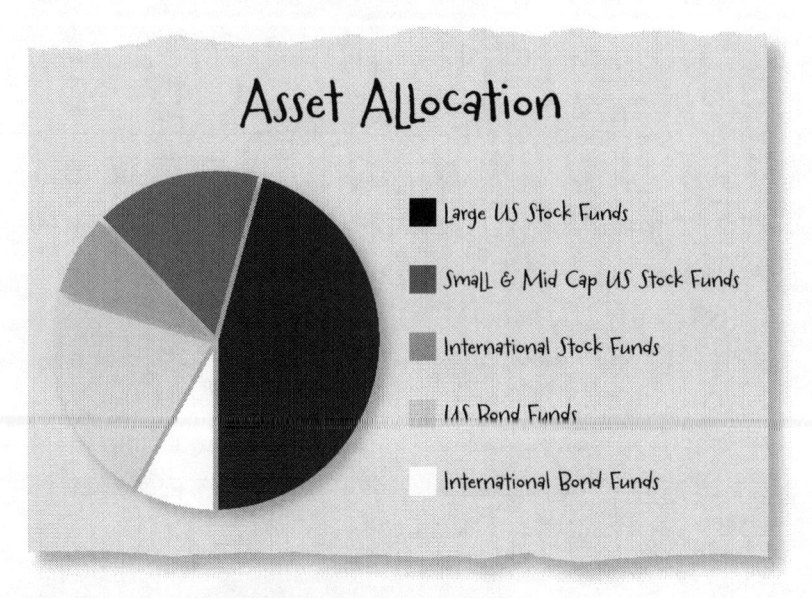

AN ASSET ALLOCATION COULD LOOK LIKE THIS—BUT DOESN'T HAVE TO

Stock Funds

* Large US Stock Funds   40 percent
* Small & Mid Cap US Stock Funds   20 percent
* International Stock Funds   10 percent

Bond Funds

* US Bond Funds   20 percent
* International Bond Funds   10 percent

Total Investment Allocation   100 percent

This is a nice, boring, diversified retirement portfolio. Your dad's portfolio might have different percentages. For example, instead of 40 percent in US Stock Funds, he may have 40 percent in US Bond Funds. Bond funds tend to be more conservative, which leads to less volatility but also less potential growth. The point is that you and your dad may own the same things but in different proportions, if you get my drift. In this example, nothing is too risky that may implode your portfolio or cause it to skyrocket overnight. That's okay. That's what we want. We are aiming for ho-hum, long-term growth and very few unexpected surprises.

TARGET YOUR DATE

Now I can't tell you what funds or ETFs (exchange traded funds) to invest in because you have a broad selection, but if you have a company retirement plan, then as I touched on in Chapter 6, you probably can pick target-date retirement funds.

A date of 2060 means you will turn sixty-five in or near the year 2060, and the funds in that portfolio reflect the suggested allocation based on your age. The target-date fund will automatically adjust every few years as you age to reduce the risk of exposure in your portfolio. If you want to set it and forget it, then this is the portfolio for you.

If you want to customize your retirement, then maybe target-date funds are not for you. For most readers, I would highly suggest the target-date series to make it easier on you. If 2060 is the recommended date for you, you can always change it to 2050 to be more conservative or 2070 to be more aggressive. The key, as always, is to start early and keep contributing.

Okay, open your eyes. Crack your knuckles, run in place, and smack the side of your head. I feel like you may have drifted off and napped a little during my investment presentation. The key is to not try and knock it out of the park with your retirement investing because history tells us slow and steady wins the race. Just like you don't want your dad to go crazy and rip off his shirt on the dance floor when he hears any '80s music. He doesn't want you to go crazy and attempt to pick the next cryptocurrency, Amazon, or Apple stock. Be boring like your old man!

$\overline{\equiv}$*GOBIT$*

GOBIT #33: Go to your HR intranet site at work and learn about your 401(k). What are the investment options? Should you use a target-date fund or pick your own funds? If you have extra money to invest after you've maxed out your retirement account, then open an investment account with a reputable firm. Consider using similar funds as your retirement account, but maybe change up the allocation so it is more in line with your short- and medium-term goals. If this process terrifies you or you have little interest, then get some guidance from a professional.

GOBIT #34: Practice investing. That's right, I said practice picking funds or ETFs or stocks, and track them for a year. Think of when you would buy an investment and then what would cause you to sell it. You don't have to be an expert, but it does help to be a student of your money. Track your practice investments on a spreadsheet each month to see how you could be doing. It can be fun in a nerdy kind of way!

I'm awesome. My hair is unbelievably stylish. I have skipped the six-pack abs and moved up to twelve-pack abs. When I'm out on the golf course, I just crush the ball down the fairway and drop in birdies like Tiger in his prime. And to top it off, I always pick the fastest TSA airport line. I am so awesome I'm thinking of taking my talents to be an online stock trader. Since stock trades are almost free now, I might as well trade as much as possible. Do you agree with my awesomeness?

Signed,

Marvelous Maverick, a.k.a. M2

Hey JB?

Dear M2,

Let me guess: you nicknamed yourself. To answer your question ... no! Cool hair, twelve-pack abs, and a questionable golf game are positives, I suppose, but that doesn't make you a stock trader. In fact, there is such a thing as overconfidence bias that can be hazardous to your portfolio when it comes to online trading, according to a research study conducted in 2021 by Daniel J. Walters and Philip M. Fernbach.[16] I'll spare you the chore of reading the lengthy study: essentially, those who traded more often performed worse because they tended to pick stocks that underperformed the market. Establish the right asset allocation for your time frame with passive funds and focus on your hair and abs. Less trading and more stomach crunches will help you in the long term.

Chapter 18

INVESTING 2.0:
This Ain't No Game

"Beer-in-hand kickball is a game.
Candyland is a game. Grand Theft Auto
is a game. Investing ain't no game!"

— Johnny B

REMINISCE WITH ME, IF YOU WILL. Remember way back when (last chapter) I introduced the riveting concepts of asset allocation and long-term investing? That's Investing 1.0 and will help you ride out the bumps and possibly grow your portfolio over the long run. I know, I know, it's boring and you want to get in the game. *C'mon, Johnny B, let me day trade the commodity markets. Flip-Cup-Coin cryptocurrency is skyrocketing; I'm going all in. Let me trade options on that dumpster fire meme stock of the week! All my buddies are in the game and crushing it.* News flash, sporto: your buddies are not crushing it!

Investing ain't no game! This also isn't online gambling. This is serious stuff. While I want you to invest for the long term in a humdrum fashion like your pop would, I understand that there will be temptations to overreach on some investments. Should you take a flier on a small tech company whose stock is under $1 per share? Is it wise to add one of seventeen thousand available cryptocurrencies to your wallet? Should you buy that two-bedroom fixer-upper condo in downtown Chicago, hoping for a turnaround? Yes, maybe, doubtful, and definitely not are the possible answers to all these questions.

In Investing 2.0, we'll explore more details about what to invest in and, more importantly, what not to invest in. Remember way back in Chapter 9 when we chatted about needs versus wants? You shouldn't buy this when you really need that! As you are pecking around online for new travel luggage and the online ad "suggests" that you explore scuba diving in Australia, focus! I'm guilty of diverted online browsing all the time, but rarely do I unleash the credit card on a purchase because, as you well know by now, I'm just too cheap. Investing your money on stuff you don't understand, you haven't researched, or that your buddy says is a "sure thing" can be catastrophic.

Y'all know Nicholas Cage, the superstar actor. He won an Oscar for his role as a drunk writer in *Leaving Las Vegas*. He starred as a treasure hunter in the *National Treasure* flicks. And my personal favorite, he nailed it as an incompetent robber in *Raising Arizona* from way back in 1987. Nic has made tens of millions over the years as a beloved actor and funnyman. Unfortunately, he also squandered most of it on cars, a collection of shrunken Pygmy heads, and a handful of castles in Germany and the United Kingdom.[17] Clearly, Nic got some bad advice along the way, or he just flat-out ignored his advisors and thought Pygmy heads were a solid investment opportunity. Today in the 2020s, you'll see Cage is making several movies a year to lift himself out of bankruptcy. Search broke actors and athletes, and you'll find hundreds of utter financial failures. Mike Tyson, Lindsay Lohan, Marvin Gaye, and the list goes on and on. *Sucks for them*, you say. *Who cares about rich celebrities who had it all and blew it?* I'm not saying you have to care; I'm saying we all can learn from their mistakes. You won't read about the hundreds of thousands of individuals who made bad investments, costing them their homes, their families, their freedom, and in some cases, their lives. On the flip side, current NBA superstar Giannis Antetokounmpo just signed a multiyear contract worth over $200 million, spreads his cash in fifty banks, and likes to go grocery shopping at night when nobody recognizes him.[18] He's probably a little too conservative for a superstar in his twenties, but he can sleep at night, so it works for him.

GAMIFICATION OF THE MARKETS

Back in 2018, a new trading platform called Robinhood came barging onto the financial world scene. As a disrupter, it offered investment trading with no transaction fees. Historically you had to pay $50 per trade if you wanted to buy/sell a stock or mutual fund. It dropped to $20, then $5, then Robinhood made all the trades free, and the other platforms had to follow along. How Robinhood makes money is a longer thesis that doesn't really matter for our discussion, but what is important is that by taking away that transaction fee, it removes one more hurdle to buying/selling that stock or fund. Is that a good thing? Suppose you're at your favorite eatery with your Lunch Bunch Friends and the waiter says the wings are free for the next ten minutes. Even though you were thinking salads, umm, yeah, that's a no-brainer, even if you're not hungry. Why pay for salads when wings are free?! Come to think of it, why even consider ordering salads when there are wings on the menu? But that's another discussion.

The same goes for buying stocks. A few trading platforms have made the trading app on your phone look like a game. As I've mentioned, it ain't no game! I'm not faulting these platforms for making trading free, but I do think making it so easy can lead to over-trading your account, which history tells us doesn't work out very well.

Back in the day, you could've gotten your stock tips from Uncle David at the Sunday family barbecue. UD would boast about how his portfolio had a bunch of "blue chip" stocks, and he just bought some IBM that is soaring. What UD didn't tell you is that he also bought a bunch of Blockbuster stock, and we all know how that turned out. Netflix ate their lunch, and they all but disappeared except for one nostalgic store in Bend, Oregon. Nowadays you can get overwhelmed with stock tips or crypto investment opportunities every time you scroll on your phone. Let's talk about some of these "opportunities."

CRYPTO OR CRYPNO

What's in your wallet? You've heard that about a gazillion times from a national bank if you've had your TV turned on this past decade. I'm more interested in what's *not* in your wallet. Crypto. Bitcoin. Ethereum. Dogecoin. Does it need to be in your investment wallet? We'll dive more into advanced placement investing in Chapter 20, but here is a bit on crypto.

A central pillar of portfolio construction is that every asset should have a purpose. For example, fixed income (a.k.a. bonds) is a diversifier and helps with tamping down the ups and downs in your portfolio. Equities (stocks) serve as an inflation hedge and offer potential long-term appreciation or growth. Cryptocurrency is an unknown volatile asset that is in its infancy. It's a baby! We don't know if crypto will replace the dollar bill as future currency to buy things or if it will be a nostalgic collectors token like the moped that is worthless in the future. According to coinmarketcap.com, as of July 2022, there are over seventeen thousand cryptocurrencies. Picking the winners is akin to having a perfect college hoops bracket during March Madness. Not going to happen! If crypto has a purpose, it is probably long-term appreciation and not short-term trading. There will be winners, but there will be thousands of losers. Buyers beware of crypto investing and limit your exposure to what you're okay with disappearing from your investment wallet. I have no clue if crypto will change the world or not, but if you *don't* have the money to lose, then I would say steer clear early in your investing life.

SHOULD YOU SPEND YOUR DAY ... TRADING?

What is day trading? Playing roulette in Vegas is gambling with bad odds because you don't know where the ball will end up. Day trading is tracking and trading different stocks or ETFs or crypto throughout the day and betting on the trend. With roulette, if the ball has ended up red seven times in a row, then it has to be black next time, right? Absolutely not! Every time the ball drops, there is a fifty-fifty chance it will be red or black. You are absolutely guessing. There is no plan. There is no pattern. There is no strategy. Blind luck, but if you get a free drink at the casino, then at least it is entertainment for an afternoon.

This is going to anger the visitors to online chat rooms, but day trading is gambling. I can't tell you how many guys (it's never gals because they're too smart) come up to me after I have a speaking engagement at a college or corporate event and say, "Dude, I've got this proven method I use to short the two-hundred-day moving average of the FTSE and then leverage up when I see an inverted hammer candle, so I can pick off the lone wolf!" What in the wide, wide world of finance are you talking about?! No, you don't have a proven method, or you'd be chillin' on a beach in the Canary Islands. Day traders are active investors who try to profit from the movement in asset prices, either up or down. Technical analysis, swing trading, hedge bets, diamond pattern, hook and ladder, and support and resistance are all terms associated with day trading. Because we now have commission-free trading, as I mentioned earlier, it makes day trading, unfortunately, easier than ever. Don't day trade! Period! Because I said so. There are professionals around the globe just waiting to pounce on novice traders and steal your hard-earned money. Just don't!

IF YOU REALLY DO HAVE EXTRA $$ TO PLAY WITH ...

I've hopefully convinced you that investing ain't no game and you should only invest in things you mostly understand and that have a proven history of solid returns. Build yourself a boring dad portfolio for your retirement and shy away from the get-rich schemes. However, let's say you start to have some extra funds and you want to roll the dice on some investment. Maybe you want to throw a few thousand at some new tech stock. Or toss a few coins at a cryptocurrency that has potential. Or start a side hustle with an espresso business aptly named Johnny's Java. I've attempted a few investments over my lifetime; a few panned out, and a few didn't. Johnny's Java was a coffee cart that we started and ran for about a year, but ironically, we were ahead of our time, and it didn't quite work out. It was a side hustle to my full-time job, and we didn't lose too much money relative to our net worth. I learned what level of risk I can tolerate and what amount of loss really stings. If you're prepared to lose every dime you invest in one of these "opportunities," then give it a go. If you are investing every last penny you have and hoping Johnny's Java carts overtake Starbucks across the country and you become a gazillionaire, then think again. It's okay to roll the dice occasionally as long as you have your financial house in order.

Ideally you could build an investment portfolio similar to your retirement account but a bit more conservative. Instead of 70 percent stock funds and 30 percent bond funds, you decide that 60 percent stock funds and 40 percent bond funds was easier to stomach. Start with $10,000 or $1,000, and add to it each month automatically. Begin with $50 a paycheck, or $500, and have it automatically transferred from your bank account to your new investment account. Start early and stay consistent. Your future self will thank you!

Let's review. Investing is serious business, and it ain't no game. Don't day trade. Ever!

GOBIT$

GOBIT #35: Knowledge is power. Patience is key. Rarely do you have to make a quick decision to invest. Practice investing. Yes, practice. If you want to understand the markets, practice buying and selling in a spreadsheet. Don't invest the money, but practice with buys, sells, information, and walking away. Track the changes in your investments each month to see how you might have done. Practice for twelve months or longer. Investing is for the long term, while speculating is for the short term.

GOBIT #36: If you want to invest in crypto or real estate, then research all you can. Read a book a week on crypto, blockchain, NFTs, real estate, or artificial intelligence. And *no*, reading chat boards on why Flip-Cup-Coin will be the next big thing doesn't count as research! The tech world changes fast. Be skeptical of everything you invest in and have a plan to buy and, more importantly, a plan to exit and get your money out.

You have probably heard of me ... Kargo Kev! I'm a TikTok phenom in the sixty-plus age group. I holler at young adults about fun money stuff while sitting in my lawn chair in my kargo shorts, high school letter jacket, black socks, and New Balance cross-trainers. Sometimes as the kids drive by, we have some friendly banter as I suggest they contribute to their 401(k)s, and they lob eggs at my house. Anyways, all in good fun. My question is: Are my cross-trainers "writeoffable" as a business expense since I'm technically a gig worker?

Thanks,

Kargo Kev

Dear Kargo Kev,

This one will take a moment to unpack. By "writeoffable," are you asking if you can deduct your 1980s cross-trainers as a business expense on your taxes? Doubtful. Cargo shorts, definitely not. But I don't want to discourage the admirable work you're doing to promote financial literacy. Computers, Wi-Fi (assuming you're not still on dial-up AOL), cell phone, and camera may have some limited writeoffability ... geez, now you have me making up words. Check with your tax accountant to see what qualifies, and keep "teaching" our youth about money no matter how many eggs hit your house.

Chapter 19

YOUR SIDE HUSTLE AND LOWERING YOUR TAXES

"When my kids turned twenty-one, I taught each one of them about taxes by drinking 33 percent of their 'first' beer."

— Johnny B

WHETHER OR NOT YOU ARE AN international icon yet, with people who handle those annoying things like taxes and doggie daycare, you should be aware of how much you are loaning to the government. Yes, I said "loaning to the government." If you think of taxes as a loan that you are giving to Uncle Sam, it may cause you to be more aware of how much you are lending him. Don't get me wrong; you won't get much of the loan back, but you can hope your government spends it wisely on stuff like schools, roads, $750 toilets, and a project to gauge the aggressiveness of hamsters in a cage match when one of them was jacked-up on steroids.[19] The government will find a way to spend it, but you can control, somewhat, how much you give to the IRS to spend each year.

AGI, exemptions, credits, deductions, AMT, lions, tigers, and bears, oh my! What the heck am I talking about? I can hear you screaming inside your head right now. You want to sink into your couch and avoid the tax talk by watching a reality show about twenty-somethings trapped in a mansion on an exotic island with too much time on their hands and no real jobs, so they can take six months off to film a reality show that is nowhere near reality. Sorry, that was dad rant #43.

What's the difference between having too much in taxes deducted from your paycheck and burying your cash in the backyard? Answer: nothing. They are both lousy ways to make your money work for you and to generate a return.

HUSTLING ON THE SIDE

But I love getting a big fat tax refund each year. It's like Christmas in April! Okay, I'll admit. It's always fun to get a big check in the mail. But you have got to think about the source of that check. You gave your government too much money every pay period in order to get that check. Would you just hand over a couple hundred bucks a week to, say, your little brother—the one who skateboards all day—just so he could give it all back to you at the end of the year? If you said "Yes," especially out loud, perhaps you should consider a more remedial book than this one. Maybe *Green Eggs and Ham* by Dr. Seuss (if it hasn't been banned yet).

I know you. You're smarter than that. You want to make the most of your earnings. One of those ways is to manage your taxes. Accounts such as 401(k)s, 403(b)s, and SEP IRAs are one of your best tax management tools. Your contributions are made pre-tax, meaning they are deducted from your gross earnings at year-end. You save approximately 25 to 30 percent in taxes on everything you contribute.

Another way to help with taxes at your young age is to get a side hustle. I'm not condoning a career where dollar bills are slipped into your waistband or you're hedging crypto assets on the Hong Kong exchange, but maybe writing a travel blog or delivering for DoorDash can close the cash flow gap. A side hustle needs to make money, or it is just a hobby. I didn't make the rules; the IRS did. But if you're making a little money, then you can add to a retirement program, save for emergencies, and write off some expenses.

YOU HAVE MY ATTENTION—HOW MIGHT THIS WORK?

I'm not giving tax advice. I'm not giving tax advice. I'm not giving tax advice. Did I make myself clear? Tax rules change every few years, so consult a professional for the latest and greatest rules. Let's say Jack the travel blogger decides to write about his excursions to Thailand, Vietnam, and Costa Rica. He posts his blog each month with pictures, interviews, and witty banter on the local customs. Jack starts to acquire more readers, in addition to his grandparents, which allows him to advertise on his website. The revenue isn't life-changing yet, but it does pay for his annual ski pass, an occasional burrito, and his unique collection of ukuleles. Does he have to pay taxes? Yes! Can he deduct some expenses to offset his taxes? Definite maybe. Let's look at some possible deductions.

* Notebooks and iPads for writing. Okay, maybe a computer or a portion of a computer that is dedicated to blog-writing time.
* Income taxes on the profits for being self-employed, as well as 15.3 percent for Medicare, FICA, and Social Security taxes. This combo takes a bite into your profits, but you can deduct half from your taxes.
* Wi-Fi and cell phone charges that are used for writing time and meetings.
* Website, editing apps, and software charges that apply to your writing.
* Airplane travel, beach resorts, camel rides, or rickshaw rides in Vietnam while writing?! This is where it gets hazy, and you'll want to consult a tax expert. You may be able to expense part of your travel, but don't ask me to be an expert witness when you get audited!

Open up a SEP (simplified employee pension) IRA and contribute pre-tax money to lower your potential taxable amount. It comes with lots of rules, but it may be a good option to increase your retirement nest egg.

DON'T GIVE IT ALL AWAY

Okay, that doesn't necessarily guarantee you won't pay taxes or get a big ole refund when you file. You can, however, either do a little math yourself or invest in a tax accountant. Unless your income fluctuates wildly throughout the year due to the variable number of clicks you get from your ad partners on your blog or your habit of switching between door-to-door window sales and commercial real estate jobs every month, you can probably come up with an accurate estimate of your total earnings, eligible deductions like your 401(k), and total taxes due at year-end. Once you have that last number, you can adjust your W-4 through your employer to mirror that number. Will it be perfect? No. The IRS is too damn sneaky and would never let you calculate an exact estimate. However, you'll end up owing just a bit (which would probably be a good sign) or get a smaller return. In the meantime, you will have more income available to invest wisely, like we learned back in Chapters 17 and 18, rather than burying dollars in a shoebox.

≡GOBIT$

GOBIT #37: Open a tax-deferred retirement account like a SEP IRA if you don't have a retirement plan through work. Then contribute as much as your accountant or tax management system says you can. SEP IRAs are usually limited to 25 percent of your earned income each year, so check the current rules.

GOBIT #38: Consider hiring a tax accountant. Yes, they come at a cost, but if you choose smartly, you can find a partner who can help you lawfully minimize your taxes and maximize your income. If you have income outside of your W-2 standard income, like a side hustle or a rental property, then a CPA can possibly save you money year after year.

My boyfriend, Weston, is passive-aggressive. Like he always has a tummy ache when I want to go see the latest rom-com at the movie theater, but the next morning, he's up at the crack of dawn to play boozy golf all day with his idiot friends. Anyways, I'm not angry or bitter, and that has nothing to do with my question; it's just a fact. More importantly, can you explain passive index funds?

Signed,

Weston's "I'm not bitter" girlfriend

Dear Not Bitter,

First, dump him. He sounds high-maintenance. Second, passive management or indexing is based on investing in exactly the same securities and in the same proportions as an index like the S&P 500. *That's interesting. Please tell me more about the S&P 500,* you ask? The S&P 500 is a market-capitalization-weighted index of the five hundred largest US publicly traded companies. Stick with me for a second! Many experts consider this index the best gauge of the US economy. You cannot invest directly in the index, but you can find funds that try to mimic its performance. The goal of passive management or investing is not to beat the market but to replicate the performance of an index as closely as possible. Contrary to popular belief, passive investing is not without risk, and you should research it thoroughly before making a decision.

Chapter 20

ADVANCED PLACEMENT FINBIT$

"Invest in yourself, and the return will
pay dividends for a lifetime."

— Johnny B

KIND OF CHEESY, but maybe it made you chuckle. Wow, you
just plowed through nineteen chapters on personal finance! Go
get a mani-pedi, have some pizza delivered, or just relish in the
sheer excitement of knowing that you have spent more time
acquiring money knowledge than 98.3 percent of your peers. I
have no idea about the exact percentage, but I'm confident you're
way ahead of your friends. Hold on to your red solo cup; we're
just getting started.

Remember when you got out of college with that communi-
cations degree after you changed majors five times and thought,
Now what? Unless you're an NFL first-round draft pick, you
realized you needed a little bit more schooling in broadcast
journalism to find your true passion. Now you have your own

murder mystery podcast, you write a travel blog with a handful of non-family followers, and your future looks amazing. The same goes for personal finance. You don't need to be an expert, but it does help to stay up on money topics to keep you on the right path.

We've gone through how to be a world-class cheapskate. Why save for emergencies. How to choose your work benefits. And finally, Investing 1.0 and 2.0. Establishing good habits with money, like choosing a salad over a burger, is the key to long-term financial health.

You will be fat. There, I said it. Maybe not offensive lineman-type large, but it's likely that you will be softer and rounder at some point in your life. Should you just throw in the towel, wear sweats 24/7, and hope the occasional weekend hike will whisk you back into shape? You can wish, but you will learn that it is up to you to put down the Double-Double Monster-Style Cheeseburger and make your own veggie protein smoothie. You can wake up and scroll through videos for thirty minutes or speed walk three miles around the neighborhood. Unlike what you may see on social media, personal wealth and a rockin' hot bod are largely up to you. Let's look at some advanced placement investment themes and whether they are right for you.

The *number one* thing to remember when investing your hard-earned money is this: If you don't understand the investment, then don't invest. I'm not saying keep your money in a shoebox buried in the back corner of your closet because for your money to grow, you need to take some risk. However, as we discussed in Chapter 17, I want you to be boring with the bulk of your investments. Too often you hear of high-profile athletes who lose their fortunes because of bad investments and bad advice. If they roll the dice on some unknown startup and lose a few million here or there, they may have the earning potential to make it back. You, me, and the rest of us mortals—probably not. Understand what you're investing in and always ask yourself, *How do I get my money out of this investment when I want to?*

SPECULATING IN PENNY STOCKS

Notice I didn't say *investing* in penny stocks; the more accurate definition is *speculating* in penny stocks. You've learned that if you are buying a standard stock, then you are buying a share of a company. When you buy Apple or Microsoft stock, you will receive a dividend each quarter as income and you hope the price increases over time. Large-company stocks can and will fluctuate over time, and the companies could even go out of business; however, they have a long history of sales and have probably navigated a few down markets. Buying stock from one company—even if it's a larger one—is still a significant risk, although if the company has been around for a few decades, it'll have a track record you can research.

A penny stock, on the other hand, refers to a small company whose shares typically trade for lower than $5 per share. Startups or companies that are very small are usually considered high-risk investments due to their low price, lack of liquidity, and small market capitalization. Translation: a penny stock doesn't trade as often as larger companies, so it may be more challenging to sell the penny stock when you want to. These companies could be drug companies that have a promising drug in the pipeline, but it still must go through the approval process, which could derail future profits. Penny stocks could also be high-flying startup tech companies that are looking to disrupt part of the economy, and interestingly enough, they don't have any sales yet!

Trading penny stocks is akin to online sports betting. It's not investing; it's gambling. You should be extremely cautious and knowledgeable about what you are buying. Don't be surprised if you buy a penny stock, the company goes out of business, and your speculation/investment is now worth zero. Bottom line ... steer clear of penny stocks.

SUSTAINABLE INVESTING

"Doing Well by Doing Good" has been the mantra of sustainable investing over the years. ESG (environmental and social governance) investing, sustainable investing, green portfolios, and impact investing are somewhat synonymous, so we aren't going to split hairs for the point of this discussion. The idea is that you can direct your investment dollars to focus on companies and funds that adhere to certain environmental and social protocols.

The early 2020s have seen an explosion of interest in ESG funds, but this sector of the investment horizon still has to add some standards so everybody claiming to be ESG is truly ESG. Buyer beware: when you focus on ESG investing, you will inevitably leave out some companies that have provided stable, long-term returns for investors, like energy companies, and this could alter your personal returns. Also, ESG investing may have an overabundance of high-tech companies in their fund, which may add to the risk when that sector is out of favor. However, ESG investing has momentum, especially with Millennials, and will evolve, so if it interests you, continue to educate yourself. Just don't put blinders on and ignore other opportunities.

LET'S GET REAL ABOUT REAL ESTATE INVESTING

Real estate investing is not for everyone, but for some, it is the only way to invest. As your wealth continues to grow, you may look for other options outside of traditional investing in the markets. Investing in real estate can certainly add to your long-term wealth, so let us explore two examples.

One option is to buy a condo in the Colorado mountains or on a lake in the Ozarks, and offer short-term weekend rentals. Assuming you have to borrow the money, you'll need to make enough rental income to cover the mortgage, HOA fees, cleaning, repairs, and management fees. The pluses are that you can get some income, tax benefits, and the personal use of a condo in the mountains. The negatives are the lack of liquidity, large down payment, the cost of covering the monthly expenses with no renters, repair headaches, and, of course, dealing with renters.

Another option is to buy a rental home in the city where you live. It has all the same benefits and challenges of a condo in the mountains but without the personal use of the property. In theory, you will have a long-term renter in the property who covers all the expenses, but if they leave or you have to boot them out because they didn't pay their rent, then you must cover the monthly expenses!

Personally, I have had multiple real estate investments over the years, and if you buy me a doughnut, I will give you my completely biased opinion of the reasons to buy and not to buy real estate. Timing is everything. Let's assume you want to get into the real estate game and buy a short-term rental condo in the Lake of the Ozarks. Below are some details to consider …

Short-term rental: Condo

Pluses	Minuses
Family use of the property	Renters damage property
Extra income	Mortgage obligation
Rental income pays down mortgage	Vacancies = lost income
Long-term appreciation	Vacations turn into workdays
Tax depreciation advantages	Not a liquid investment

This is a short list of items to think about, and it is up to you if the positives outweigh the negatives. I've known folks who have turned one Airbnb into multiple Airbnb properties, and that has provided a generous stream of income for them. On the flip side, I've had friends who went too big too fast, and the income didn't cover their expenses. They eventually had to sell a few properties at a tremendous discount just to get some cash flow. Start small and see if the short-term rental real estate game is for you.

Another option is to buy a condo or single-family home with the idea of renting it out yearly or longer. We attempted this strategy when we bought a rental house in the mid-2000s with the idea of having long-term renters cover the mortgage and the miscellaneous costs. Again, timing is everything. It was a great location near downtown Littleton, Colorado, but it was an old property that needed a lot of fixing up. We painted every wall, added carpet and hardwood floors, updated the kitchen, repaired the roof, landscaped the yard, and replaced every window. I had four renters over five years of ownership, and three of them were awful. While I liked owning and working on the property, I learned I was not cut out to deal with tenants. If I had a management team to handle the tenants, it would have made my life easier, but the cheapskate in me didn't want to pay the fees. Bad choice! We eventually sold the house for a modest profit, and I was thrilled to be out of the landlord business.

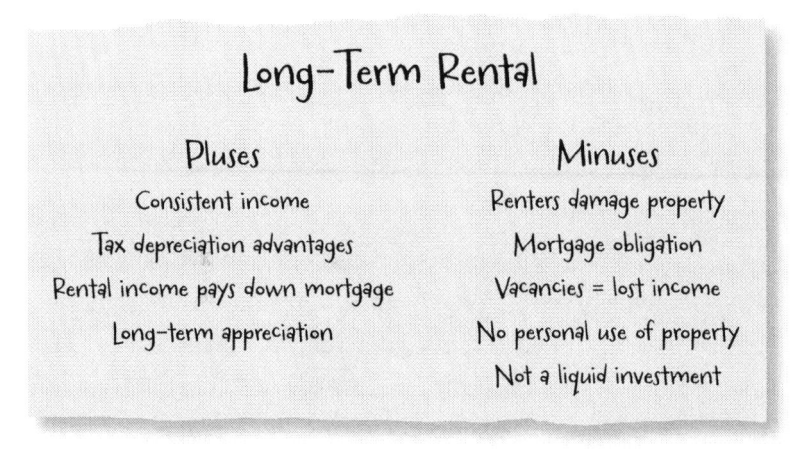

Long-Term Rental

Pluses	Minuses
Consistent income	Renters damage property
Tax depreciation advantages	Mortgage obligation
Rental income pays down mortgage	Vacancies = lost income
Long-term appreciation	No personal use of property
	Not a liquid investment

The goal of real estate investing is to acquire good properties with consistent income and the potential for long-term appreciation. As with all investments, I'd find a good mentor who knows the real estate game. Read all you can and be patient and cautious with your investments.

CRYPTO, BLOCKCHAIN, NFTS, METAVERSE, AND WHATEVER IS NEXT

And last but certainly not least in your advanced investment curriculum is the Wild, Wild West of cryptocurrencies. Unless you've been yurt camping in the Rocky Mountains for a decade, you've heard of bitcoin. You've probably heard of blockchain, NFTs, and the impending metaverse, too. It would take a "few" chapters at a minimum to go through each definition, and I'm not sure the investing community even knows what to do with this new sleeve of speculating. Simply put, crypto is very, very interesting but also very, very early. As I've said, if you buy a cryptocurrency or NFT, you are not investing; you are speculating. Investing involves setting a goal, deciding how much risk to take, choosing the best path to reach that goal, and then building a well-diversified portfolio to try to attain that goal. Speculating is putting cash into a single stock, cryptocurrency, or new technology with the hope of quick returns.

Don't kid yourself when Owen in the next cubicle says, "Dude, you have to buy some of this METAcoin. I've got the inside track on it, and it is only forty-three cents a share and it is blowing up!" Run, don't walk, away from Owen, and refrain from discussing anything financial with him again. You may love Owen's taste in EDM, but I'd avoid his taste in "investing." We've talked about personal finance and making good decisions for twenty chapters, so you can't convince me that dumping all your money into one of seventeen thousand-plus cryptocurrencies is a sound investment.

However, crypto is something. Blockchain is something. Smart contracts are something. I'm not sure we know what they are yet, but they could revolutionize banking, healthcare, and other industries. The challenge is knowing who is going to be the winner. We don't know. Nobody knows! Early in the development of the car industry, there were over two thousand auto manufacturers. Not many auto companies are left these days, as most went out of business or were swallowed up by competitors. What I'm preaching on my Dad porch is, again, buyer beware. It is okay to speculate, but be prepared to lose every dime you invest. It might work out, but early adoption can be detrimental to your long-term portfolio.

GOBIT$

GOBIT #39: Listen to a highly entertaining and educational financial podcast like my **FINBIT$** *with Johnny B* (shameless plug) that will keep your money brain in tune. With my podcast, you might learn something and chuckle at the same time, but if you listen to almost any financial education podcast, you are ahead of the curve.

GOBIT #40: Read a personal finance book each month. I know you would rather give a speech naked in front of your high school reunion, but don't completely bury your head in the sand and forget about your finances. Be a skeptic when you read a book, finance article, or chat room banter, and keep your money mind sharp!

GOBIT #41: Take a personal finance 101 class at the local college or online. I'm sorry that your high school and college didn't require you to take this critical class, but now you can do it on your own. I've taught a personal finance college course for years, and it will give you a good foundation for your financial future.

GOBIT #42: You know the book club that you kind of attend but you really just drink wine? Or the gym where you walk around and scrutinize the equipment but never actually get much exercise? Try turning this valuable time with friends into an opportunity to talk about anything financial. Just bring up one topic. You'd be amazed at how much you have in common.

AND THAT'S ALL
I HAVE TO SAY
ABOUT THAT!

YOU'RE DONE. Well actually, you've just started on your path to financial freedom. Sounds kind of corny, but you really are in control at this point in your life. I could write a long wrap-up, but I don't want you to chuck this book into the river. Maybe it sits on your bedside table. Possibly you toss it in your backpack to glance at on occasion. Maybe you'll bring up a few **FINBIT$** to your friends the next time you're zipping around town on scooters. Don't be selfish; share your newfound wisdom with your buddies.

As I said way back at the beginning of this financial journey, you will encounter many, if not all, of these financial conundrums, so use this book as a reference tool when you need to start making those adult decisions. You'll probably have to do more research or seek out a financial professional, but take control when it's time to make decisions about money.

Now go make your dad proud and blaze your trail toward financial independence!

ACKNOWLEDGMENTS

FOR THOSE OF YOU WHO HAVE WRITTEN a book or attempted to write a book, you understand it is not a solo project. Sure, sometimes you have to hide out in a coffee shop, on a plane ride, or in a corner of the library with your headphones on and just start pounding on the keyboard. Once you get in the groove of writing, it seems to flow, but pulling it into a cohesive book that someone other than your mom might want to read is a team effort.

First, I need to thank and apologize to my three great kids. You have allowed me, sometimes unwillingly, to poach your stories about life and money as a young adult to create a teaching moment for others your age. Jack, my boy, has had to endure my liberal use of his financial experiences to write anecdotes that others might find humorous and hopefully educational. Thank you, Junior. You get a complimentary autographed copy and a pint of your choice! Next, I need to thank my middle child, Ellie, who seems to be evolving into quite the smartass like her pop.

Only she's smart and sometimes I'm just an ass. Anyway, thanks, Sweetie, for your stories, feedback, and promotional efforts with your friends. You also get a complimentary autographed copy and a fancy latte of your choice! And finally, thank you to my Baby Kate. I am so glad you have the artistic talent to help with the sketches because the rest of the family has zero talent. You were able to create great pictures out of my chicken scratch, and I really appreciate it. You also get a complimentary autographed copy, and I'll fill up your gas tank before you go back to college!

I'd like to thank my publishing team; without them, I'd just have a bunch of ideas on Word docs that didn't make any sense. Let me first thank my longtime writing partner, tennis partner, and overall word therapist ... Ron Lamberson. He is a best-selling novelist with his The Kilimanjaro Club series, which includes the book A *Grave Invitation*. Since Ron is a seasoned writer and a smartass, he was a tremendous help when I needed a new idea, a revised paragraph, or just a catchy phrase. I appreciate it very much, buddy, and you will receive a signed book and maybe even a glossy eight-by-ten photo of me for your office! Alexandra, my editor, thankfully got my sense of dad humor and was a tremendous help in pulling together the chapters and keeping the project moving to completion. My designer, Victoria, made the book cover and interior eye-catching yet simple and easy to read. And finally, Kirsten, my project manager and coach, held me accountable, politely nagged me, and made sure all the little things got done! Thank you so much to my team.

Throughout the book, you'll see countless people's names that I used for examples or to get the point across. Every name is a family member of mine, whether it be siblings, nephews, nieces, parents, and in-laws, and I certainly took some creative license in the examples to emphasize a point. No major harm done; I hope they all know I like to tease! I have many cheapskates on both sides of my family, so there was no shortage of material from Papa Den, Uncle Dan, and Uncle David, all the way down to my nephew Owen, who might be the thriftiest of us all. Thanks for being tightwads.

And last but not least, I want to thank my beautiful wife, Carey. If I didn't have you in my corner as my partner, wife, and best friend, I would not have finished this project. The times you locked me in my office until I wrote a chapter or withheld a cookie reward until I finished editing a section were the tough love I needed. Thank you, honey, and hopefully we can travel the country together in our future Sprinter van, teaching young adults about money!

APPENDICES

APPENDIX A
Personal Balance Sheet

JANUARY			
What you Own (Assets)		**What You Owe (Liabilities)**	
Cash in Bank		Personal Loan from Grandma	
Work Retirement Account—401(k), 403(b)		Student Loan(s)	
Roth IRA		Credit Card Balance (DON'T let this happen)	
2020 Toyota 4Runner		Car Loan	
House or Townhome		Mortgage	
Vintage Xbox			
Mountain Bike			
Shoe Collection			
iPad, iPhone, MacBook			
Total Assests	$0.00	Total Liabilities	$0.00
Assets – Liabilities = Net Worth $			

APPENDIX B

Personal Income Statement

INCOMING	MONTHLY	OUTGOING	MONTHLY
Salary		Rent	
Interest		Groceries	
Side Hustle		Entertainment	
Dividends		Student Loan Payments	
Other		Taxes	
		Car (Gas, Maintenance, Loan)	
		401(k) Savings	
Total			
What's left over each month?		$7,500 - $6,600 =	

APPENDIX C
Budget Spreadsheet

NOT ANOTHER LECTURE

1. Savings Goals	Budgeted
Emergency Savings	
Short-Term Savings Goal	
Long-Term Savings Goal	
Retirement Account	
Other	
Occasional Expenses (Tab 2)	
Total Savings Goals	$0.00

2. Debt Payments	
Mortgage	
Student Loan	
Auto Loan	
Credit Card	
Other	
Other	
Other	
Total Debt Payments	$0.00

3. Bills and Utilities	
Rent (if no mortgage)	
Electricity	
Natural Gas	
City/County Utilities	
Phone (cell/landline)	
Internet/Cable/Satellite	
Other	
HOA/Repairs	
Other	
Insurance/Medical	
Automobile Insurance	
Life Insurance	
Disability Insurance	
Long-Term Care	
Physician Copayments	
Prescriptions	
Other	
Give Back	
Charity	
Other	
Total Bills and Utilities	$0.00

TOTAL Income	$0.00
TOTAL Expenses	
Available to Budget	

Income	Budgeted
Income 1	
Income 2	
Income 3	
Other	
Other	
Total Income	$0.00

3. Variable Living Costs	
Groceries	
Fast Food	
Gas for Car	
Ride-share Services, Tolls, and Parking	
Clothes	
Dry Cleaning	
Exercise/Gym	
Toiletries/Makeup	
Haircuts	
Childcare	
Pet Care	
Other	
Other	
Other	
Total Variable Living Costs	$0.00

3. Variable Living Costs	
Personal Spending 1	
Personal Spending 2	
Entertainment	
Dates/Outings	
Movies/Music	
Hobbies	
Vacation	
Lessons/Education	
Memberships	
Subscriptions	
Christmas	
Gifts	
Other	
Total Fun Money	$0.00

ENDNOTES

1   Fidelity Brokerage Services LLC, "The Fidelity Investments Millennial Money Study," 2014, https://www.fidelity.com/bin-public/060_www_fidelity_com/documents/fidelity/millennial-money-study.pdf.

2   Marcel Schwantes, "Science says 92 Percent of People Don't Achieve Their Goals. Here's How the Other 8 Percent Do," Inc., July 26, 2016, https://www.inc.com/marcel-schwantes/science-says-92-percent-of-people-dont-achieve-goals-heres-how-the-other-8-perce.html.

3   Patrick R. Heck, et al., "65% of Americans believe they are above average in intelligence: Results of two nationally representative surveys," July 3, 2018, PLoS One, doi: 10.1371/journal.pone.0200103, https://www.ncbi.nlm.nih.gov/pmc/articles/PMC6029792/.

4   Economic Research Service, "Food Prices and Spending," US Department of Agriculture, Last updated January 6, 2023, accessed February 13, 2023, https://www.ers.usda.gov/data-products/ag-and-food-statistics-charting-the-essentials/food-prices-and-spending/.

5   Carmen Reinicke, "56% of Americans can't cover a $1,000 emergency expense with savings," CNBC, January 19, 2022, https://www.cnbc.com/2022/01/19/56percent-of-americans-cant-cover-a-1000-emergency-expense-with-savings.html.

6   Tyler Schmall, "US shoppers can't stop impulse spending," New York Post, February 21, 2018, https://nypost.com/2018/02/21/us-shoppers-cant-stop-impulse-spending/.

7   "Most Millennials Put Travel Above Buying a Home or Paying Off Debt," Travel + Leisure, November 10, 2016, https://www.yahoo.com/lifestyle/most-millennials-put-travel-above-140006360.html.

8   Chris Katje, "If You Bought $1,000 In Apple Stock When The iPod Was Released, Here's How Much You'd Have Now," Benzinga, September 11, 2022, https://www.benzinga.com/general/education/22/05/27264183/if-you-bought-1-000-in-apple-stock-when-the-ipod-was-released-heres-how-much-youd-have-now).

9   National Archives, "Social Security Act (1935)," accessed July 15, 2022, https://www.archives.gov/milestone-documents/social-security-act.

10   IRS, "Retirement Plans," IRS.gov, accessed February 14, 2023, https://www.irs.gov/retirement-plans.

11   Bankrate, "Average credit card interest rates," CreditCards.com, accessed February 14, 2023, https://www.creditcards.com/news/rate-report/.

12   Joe Resendiz, "Average credit card debt in America: 2021," LendingTree, updated February 24, 2022, https://www.valuepenguin.com/average-credit-card.

13   Head Topics, "People are spending $886 million on Valentines for their pets," February 14, 2019, https://headtopics.com/us/people-are-spending-886-million-on-valentines-for-their-pets-4222298.

14   Renee Bennett, "Should couples have a separate or joint bank account?" Bankrate, February 16, 2023, https://www.bankrate.com/banking/reasons-for-married-couples-to-consider-separate-bank-accounts/.

15   Wijnand A. P. van Tilburg, Eric R. Igou, and Mehr Panjwani, "Boring People: Stereotype Characteristics, Interpersonal Attributions, and Social Reactions, Sage Journals, accessed July 13, 2022, https://journals.sagepub.com/doi/10.1177/01461672221079104.

16   Daniel J Walters, "Investor memory of past performance is positively biased and predicts overconfidence," PNAS, September 2, 2021, https://www.pnas.org/doi/10.1073/pnas.2026680118.

17   Emmie Martin, "Nicolas Cage blew $150 million on a dinosaur skull, pygmy heads and 2 European castles," CNBC, August 9, 2019, https://www.cnbc.com/2019/08/09/why-nicholas-cage-blew-150-million-dollars-on-a-dinosaur-skull-and-two-castles.html.

18   Ariel Zilber, "Bucks star Giannis Antetokounmpo has money in 50 different bank accounts," NY Post, April 8, 2022, https://nypost.com/2022/04/08/bucks-star-giannis-antetokounmpo-has-money-in-50-bank-accounts/; Mike D. Sykes, II, "Giannis Antetokounmpo was pleasantly surprised nobody recognized him on a late night trip to the grocery store," September 30, 2021, FTW USA Today, https://ftw.usatoday.com/2021/09/giannis-antetokonmpo-bucks-grocery-shopping.

19   Ruth I Wood, et al., "'Roid rage in rats? Testosterone effects on aggressive motivation, impulsivity and tyrosine hydroxylase," Physiology & Behavior (Feb. 17, 2013), doi:10.1016/j.physbeh.2012.12.005.

ABOUT THE AUTHOR

JOHNNY BOHAN is the founder and CEO of FinBits Media LLC, a personal financial media company. He is a personal finance humorist, a college professor, Dad of three twenty-somethings, husband, wealth advisor, speaker, podcaster, and financial blogger. As a Certified Financial Planner™ professional, his goal is to bring simplicity, education, and  humor to the complex and confusing world of personal finance. Throughout his fifteen years as a financial advisor and entrepreneur, Johnny has always had a passion for educating his clients and their kids about how to make good financial decisions and, more importantly, how to avoid making financial blunders.

Johnny was a student at the University of Kansas School of Business in the late 1980s, and his journey in personal finance led him to become an advocate for teaching personal finance to young adults to get them started off on the right path. He has been an Affiliate Professor in Personal Finance at Metro State University in Denver. He has taught at The Leeds School of Business at the University of Colorado and has been a featured speaker at colleges throughout the Rocky Mountain region and the Western US. He is the author of *finbit$*, a biweekly financial education blog that attempts to educate the masses about money topics in a lighthearted tone. He is also the host of the financial podcast *Finbit$ with Johnny B*, where he interviews Millennials and Gen Zers to guide them with their financial questions in an educational and humorous dad kind of way.

www.johnnypbohan.com

Finbits with Johnny B podcast

Contact : Johnny@johnnypbohan.com

Made in the USA
Middletown, DE
05 November 2023

41902109R00137